LIVING RICH

HOW TO LIVE AS WELL AS A BILLIONAIRE ON A MIDDLE-CLASS BUDGET

By Mark Morgan Ford

Published by:
Cap & Bells Press
New York, New York

www.capandbellspress.com

This book is based on essays by Mark Morgan Ford from three sources: (1) *Early to Rise*, a newsletter that he wrote from 2000 to 2010, (2) *Creating Wealth*, a newsletter that he currently writes, and (3) the Wealth Builders Club of *The Palm Beach Letter*.

Creating Wealth is a monthly newsletter that provides beginning to advanced strategies for generating extra income and accumulating wealth. It is free for subscribers to *The Palm Beach Letter*.

The Palm Beach Letter is a general circulation publication that aims to provide its subscribers with useful advice about building wealth, living well, and investing. For more information, visit www.palmbeachletter.com.

Table of Contents

Part II: Developing a Rich Mind

Introduction

When you think about the rich—the really rich—you may find yourself marveling at their... well, their money.

Take Bill Gates, one of the world's richest men. If you think $10 million is a fortune, consider this: He has 5,000 of them. If he put his money in $1,000 bills, he'd have 50 million of them!

How great could you live if you were as rich as he?

You could have the perfect home, drive luxury cars, enjoy all of your favorite toys, eat the most delicious meals, and take the most amazing vacations... and you'd never worry about money!

Sounds good, right?

But do you really need $50 billion to enjoy that kind of lifestyle? Wouldn't $50 million do just as well?

Of course it would. So would $25 million.

Hmmm. Something is going on here that we need to think about. On the one hand, there is no doubt that you need a significant amount of money to live like a billionaire. On the other hand, it may be much less than you would expect.

My Aha! Moment

It so happens that I've been thinking about this for years. It began on a vacation in Rome when. I was fifty years old. I should have simply enjoyed exploring the city with my wife, K. Instead, I couldn't stop running business and financial plans through my head. It made me wonder why I was still caught up in this quest for more money. "How much do I really need in order to have everything I could possibly want?" I asked myself.

The answer was easy: I already had enough money. More than enough. Yet I was still chasing wealth. And I wasn't really enjoying it. I realized that I couldn't enjoy it precisely because I was chasing it. It was an obvious irony that had, until that moment, eluded me.

So as we were passing over a bridge that crossed the Tiber, I decided that increasing my wealth would no longer be a goal of mine. From then on, I would focus on getting the most out of every thing and every experience that I was fortunate enough to have.

And that is exactly what I did. But first, I had to figure out what, exactly, gave me the greatest pleasure.

As it turns out, this was a two-stage process… beginning with the material things.

Part I

Material Things—Having the Best That Money Can Buy

Chapter 1

Living Rich Is All About Spending Wisely

In this book, I am going to prove to you that—if you are willing to do some careful thinking and make wise decisions—you can live just as well as Bill Gates on a fraction of his income.

Let's start with this: With respect to acquiring material things, what advantage does great wealth provide?

The most obvious answer is that great wealth allows you to buy whatever you want. The price of anything is no longer a barrier. With that barrier removed, you could easily own the finest material things.

That sounds like a significant benefit. But there are two problems with that thinking.

First, just because you can *afford* to buy something that is expensive doesn't mean you will enjoy it. You might one day, for example, be able to afford a yacht. But if you get seasick (as I do), owning a yacht isn't likely to give you any pleasure.

And even with something that you do enjoy—say, a fine timepiece—buying the most expensive one doesn't mean you are buying the best.

Let me give you a few more examples.

Driving Like a Billionaire

The most expensive sedan in the world (as I write this) is a Maybach Landaulet. It has a 12-cylinder turbocharged engine that reaches a top speed of 155 miles per hour. Its price tag: $1.4 million.

I could afford to buy a Landaulet. But I don't own one. Why? Because it isn't—in my opinion—the best sedan in the world. There are at least a half-dozen that are better than the Landaulet, and most of them are less than half the price.

My personal choice for "best sedan in the world" is the BMW 760Li.

Like the Landaulet, the BMW 760Li has a 12-cylinder turbocharged engine that reaches a top speed of 155 miles per hour. Plus, it is better looking, better designed, more reliable—and it drives like… well, you'd have to come over and try out my car to understand.

You can buy a new BMW 760Li for $140,000 or a used one with 40,000 miles on it (barely broken in) for less than $40,000. The BMW will run like a top for twenty years and look elegant throughout its lifetime.

The Landaulet will start to look foolish the moment you drive it out of the showroom. (Car experts will know that you don't know squat about cars.) And it will look sillier every year thereafter as you plow tens of thousands of dollars into it to keep it going. Amortizing a $40,000 BMW over twenty years means you are paying something like $170 per month to own it. That's the same price you'd pay for a new Hyundai.

In other words, you could be driving the best sedan in the world for about $170 per month. So why aren't you?

This is the sort of dialog I want to have with you in this book.

Sleeping Like a Billionaire

What is the one thing, besides working, that you spend the most time doing?

If you are like most people, the answer is sleeping. We all know how important a good night's sleep is. People who sleep well are happier, healthier, and even wealthier. (Studies prove it.)

So what does a billionaire want out of his sleep time? I'd say the same thing you do: blissful, uninterrupted unconsciousness. And what will give you that (besides peace of mind, which you can't buy)?

Answer: a great mattress!

If you were a billionaire, you could buy the most expensive mattress in the world. But is the most expensive mattress necessarily the best? You already know the answer to that question.

Dressing Like a Billionaire

What does it cost to dress like the world's richest people? Not much—if you can forget about buying brand names at expensive stores. But to do that, you have to think about what clothes mean to you and what you want from them.

I'll explain how to do it and how to make all of your clothes-buying decisions simple. Your closet will be full of nothing but clothes that make you feel rich and comfortable. It won't be crowded, as it is now, with clothes that make you look and feel… well… less than rich and comfortable.

The Point Is This…

Contrary to popular opinion, most of the best material things in life are affordable. They are not always cheap—quality never is—but they are almost always within the financial reach of middle-class wage earners. So in the first part of this book, we will be determining what quality means and identifying the best products and where and how to acquire them.

If you buy them selectively and use them with care, you can enjoy a life as materially rich as Bill Gates on an income that wouldn't get him through lunch.

Chapter 2

The Rich Man's Home: Finding It

Bob (not his real name), my nearby neighbor, lives in a 15,000-square-foot house built in 1992. It has seven bedrooms, nine bathrooms, a two-bedroom guesthouse, and a garage that can accommodate six cars and a stretch limousine.

On the south lawn stands an immense gazebo—such as you might expect to find in a town plaza. Beside the tennis court, manmade grottos and streams feed an Olympic-sized swimming pool surrounded by limestone goddesses.

The façade of the house has two-story ionic columns supporting a porch that overlooks the beach. Everything—from the perimeter walls to the roof tiles to the statuary—is white.

Bob's house is huge. It is imposing. From the outside, it says, "I spent millions on this house. More than you will probably earn in your lifetime. Aren't you impressed?"

But it is in one important way poor. I'll get to that in a bit.

Sheila (not her real name), a friend who lives a few blocks away, has a 1,400-square-foot clapboard-sided bungalow built in 1940. It has two bedrooms, a vintage kitchen, and a screened-in porch on the side looking onto an English garden. Even from the outside, Sheila's house says, "I've spent years making this my own. Would you like to know me?"

It is small. It is friendly. And it feels rich.

The house you live in has an enormous effect on your quality of life. It is where you spend most of your time, where you raise your family, and where you entertain friends.

Your house is the haven you return to after working, where you enjoy family meals, exchange gossip, conjure up dreams, and make love. It is also a place where you keep your favorite books and display art and family photographs and travel souvenirs.

Your house is your home—your headquarters, a shelter and a retreat. It is where you can or should spend most of your best time.

Your house may also be your most expensive single possession. Whether you own it outright, have a mortgage, or rent it, your house is a significant part of your budget.

In terms of living rich, then, your house is at or near the top of the list.

Cost of Use: A Wise Way to Think About Owning Things

Many people believe that owning a house is always financially better than renting one. They point out that when you own a house, you get the benefit of price appreciation.

"Why should I fork over several thousand dollars per month in rent if, at the end of the day, I have nothing to show for it?" they say.

To arrive at the right answer to this question you must understand a concept I call "cost of use." By cost of use I mean the full cost of any non-consumable good over a period of time. Cost of use can be applied to cars, boats, planes, lawn chairs, silverware, writing instruments and, yes, houses.

Right now, for example, I'm shopping for an apartment in New York City. K and I are looking for a pied-à-terre in downtown Manhattan so we can be close to two of our sons who live in Brooklyn. I could afford to buy the apartments we are looking at. But because I now think in terms of the cost of use, I'm pretty sure that would be a bad deal.

A bit of arithmetic will demonstrate what I mean.

(In the following example, and in others that follow, I'm going to use numbers that may be true or may be invented to simplify the math. Please don't judge me by them!)

The apartments we are looking at are in the $1.3 million to $1.7 million range. So let's assume that I buy one for $1.5 million and hold onto it for ten years. What would be the cost of use on a yearly basis?

The first step is easy. We take the $1.5 million price and subtract it from the net price I think I'd be able to sell it for in ten years. Assuming an annual appreciation of 4 percent, the apartment would be worth $2,220,000. I would stand to make a profit (a capital gain) of $660,000.

That's an argument for ownership.

But now I have to figure in the cost of plunking down $1.5 million in cash—the money I would have made by investing that same $1.5 million in another investment or group of investments. Assuming I could get a 4 percent yield on that $1.5 million, it would be a wash at the end of the ten years.

Okay, so far it's a tie.

Now let's look at the other costs of ownership.

When you own real estate, you have property taxes. From what I've seen so far, I'd be paying about 1.5 percent on the appraised value of the apartment. The appraised value would very likely be the price I paid for it. So that is a cost of $22,500 per year.

Then you have association fees. The apartments I'm looking at average about $35,000 per year.

And then there is insurance and maintenance. I'm estimating that will run me $22,500 per year.

So the total cost of owning that apartment would be $80,000 per year.

Now let's look at renting.

You would think that if the rental market were "efficient," rental costs would amount to about the same thing: $80,000 per year. In fact, because of factors we don't need to discuss here, it would cost me less than that to rent one of these apartments. My best guess is that it would cost me between $4,500 and $5,000 per month, including fees.

Bottom line: It would be about $20,000 per year cheaper to rent one of these apartments than to buy. Over a ten-year period, that's a savings of $200,000.

So, in this case, renting would be the better choice.

You can do the same analysis with cars. Rather than pretending that the sticker price of that Mustang you want is the cost of owning it, consider all of the costs, including insurance, gas, maintenance, and depreciation (i.e., cost versus resale value). Then make a realistic judgment about how many years you will keep it. And then you will have your annual cost of use.

This will make it very easy for you to compare leasing (renting) versus owning. You won't make the mistake of thinking that either the sticker price or the monthly lease rate is your cost. You will make smarter decisions and have fewer regrets.

Understanding the cost of use has saved me hundreds of thousands of dollars (if not millions). It was a big, big eye-opener for me. I hope it does the same for you.

What Makes a Home "Rich"?

About a year after he moved in, Bob invited me to stop by his immense, white house for a "cook's tour." I was delighted to go, wondering whether the impression I had of him, formed by my reaction to the exterior of his house, would be validated by the interior design and furnishings. I was also eager to get to know this mysterious, rich neighbor.

I wasn't sure what to expect as he ushered me into the foyer, but I did expect to see lots of space. There would be more space. Lots of it. But not in the foyer. Instead, I found myself standing just six feet away from an oversized rococo-styled elevator.

Bob saw my face and took my expression of shock as one of awe. "Isn't it fantastic?" he asked proudly. "I bought it from a hotel in Florence. Guess how much it cost!"

"Gee, I don't know, Bob. Thirty grand?"

"No way! It cost me $150,000!"

I studied his face. There was no irony there—just a beguiling, childlike pride. I felt at once horrified and ashamed of myself. I brought a smile to my lips.

"A hundred and fifty? That's amazing. Congratulations!"

The entire tour was like that. Everything was oversized and garish and stupidly expensive. Nothing was comfortable, clever, or personal. It was all designer-selected by someone who must have been not just aesthetically illiterate but emotionally unbalanced. It was meant to impress. And it did.

But not as Bob had intended. My feeling was, "You poor, dumb fellow. You've been boondoggled and hornswoggled."

Back to Sheila's house…

The inside is a model of proportion and taste, just like the outside. Art and objects of art, carvings and prints—mementos from her world travels—as well as hundreds of books she's actually read, books that helped make her what she is, fill every room.

I remember the first time I saw it. Sheila didn't say much as she led me from one room to the next, but I kept stopping her to ask questions.

"That's a very cool piano. How old is it?"… "I see you like Haitian art. Have you been to Haiti?"… "I'm surprised to see all those books on astronomy. What's that about?"

During that one brief visit, I learned a great deal about Sheila—things that made me realize what an interesting person she is. But my questions only scratched the surface. There were a dozen things in every room that I wanted to know more about.

My tour of Bob's house taught me much less about Bob. I learned that he is a nice person who became very wealthy and then spent his money foolishly.

Bob spent more than $10 million on a house that tells me he is "living poor." Sheila spent a tiny fraction of that on a house that tells me she is "living rich."

From a Mud Hut...

I have lived in a three-room mud hut in Africa, an old townhouse in a bad neighborhood in Washington, D.C., a starter home in West Boca Raton, Florida, and a four-bedroom custom-built house in a gated community in East Boca… all before moving to my current house, a renovated Mediterranean-style compound across from the ocean in Delray Beach.

I've enjoyed all of my homes. But I have never forgotten a thought I had while sitting on the porch of that three-room mud hut in N'Djamena. It was late afternoon. A sun-shower was pelting the trees, rainwater was cascading over our tin roof. On my cassette player: Mozart's *Adagio in B Minor*. Suddenly, a monkey scampered out of the rain and sat beside me, unperturbed by my presence, waiting for the rain to stop.

The thought was: "Someday you will have a big, fancy house in a fancy neighborhood. But you will never live in a better home than this."

It wasn't just the view of our rain-soaked garden or the friendly intrusion of my primate cousin. It wasn't just knowing that I lived in a community of interesting people who cared for one another and that I could get to work in fifteen minutes on my bike and that K and I were safe.

It was the fact that this little house with its outdoor kitchen and cold-water shower met all of our needs. It met them perfectly because of who we were at that time.

In the thirty years since then, I have thought a good deal about what makes for a rich life. I have ideas, which I'll be sharing with you, but I also have a conclusion that I want to discuss now: *Living rich has little or nothing to do with how much a house costs.*

Newer and Bigger: The Habit of Home Ownership in America

In the "old days" in the U.S., people better understood the idea of a house as home. (This is true in some countries in Europe today.) People kept their houses for lifetimes—sometimes for generations. They updated them as their circumstances changed and improved them in countless little ways. These homes appreciated in value—financial and personal—as each year passed.

At the end of World War II, the idea of a house as home changed. Because of the need to accommodate hundreds of thousands of returning soldiers and their young families, a new kind of house—houses that were built quickly and meant to last fewer than fifty years—was invented. They were small and cheap, and they were all pretty much the same.

As the economy improved and families grew, the idea of "moving up" from a "starter house" to a "better" one replaced the old idea of gradually updating the house you had. A significant raise in salary was an opportunity to get out of the old house (which was already showing signs of wear) and into one that was newer and bigger.

The preference for new and big made sense for people in those post-World War II houses. Within ten years, the typical young couple had three or four children. The house they "needed" then had a larger kitchen and more bedrooms. And if it was new, that meant no need for reroofing and repainting—good reasons to justify the purchase.

But these second houses were, like the starter houses, pretty much indistinguishable from one another. A typical development of 300 houses might have four or five "models," each with an identical floor plan and all with similar landscaping. And, like the starter houses, they were not built to last.

When the markets were blazing in the 1980s, the newly rich began buying oversized million-dollar houses. Once again, most of them were in developments that offered models in several "classic" styles: perhaps a French chateau, an Italian villa, and a British manor house. But these houses were not made of timber and stone and plaster. Construction crews built them with two-by-fours and drywall. And, once again, they were meant to fall apart in thirty or forty years.

The point of this little history is to highlight the fact that most Americans today don't think of their homes as intergenerational habitats. They think of them the way people learned to think about houses in the 1950s: as temporary structures that would do until they could afford to buy something bigger and newer.

Bigger and newer. Those are the primary values of U.S. home buyers. And that is why most of the houses in any upscale suburb are identical—oversized and largely empty of the personalities of the human beings who live in them.

How Home Ownership Should Be

Your home should be a place that gives you constant pleasure. You should love everything about it—from its architecture and landscaping to its interior spaces and furnishings.

You should enjoy spending time in every part of your garden and in every room—in the kitchen and living areas, in every bedroom, and even in the bathrooms and closets!

The maintenance and upkeep of your home should not be, as it is for many, nothing but an expense and a hassle. It should be a happy, ongoing project for you—a work of art that you continue to refine and reshape.

Ideally, your home should be big enough to accommodate the favorite activities of everyone in your family, adults and children. When you are starting out, you can't expect to be able to afford a house with that kind of space. But if you "move on up," as people tend to do, you will one day have a house that at least has the potential. When that happens, I would urge you to consider making that your permanent home.

The reason I say that is because the financial value of a house—and this is true for just about every significant material good that you have—is greatly affected by how long you use it.

Moving from one house to a "better" one every three or four years may feel like progress. But I'm going to argue that at some point you need to step off this escalator of spending and start to enjoy the benefits of long-term possession.

In other words, to optimize the value of your home, you should not think of it as temporary. You should keep it as long as you can. (This, as you will see, is an overarching principle of "living rich.")

An Argument for "Staying Put"

Keeping a home for a long period of time gives you the best chance of seeing its monetary value appreciate. The rate at which its dollar value goes up compounds over time, just as it does with any other investment. If you've ever looked at a compounding graph, you know what I mean. For the first ten years, the appreciation is meager. From ten to twenty years, it is interesting. As you approach forty years, it becomes astronomical.

Another financial benefit of keeping your home for a long time is that it gives you a chance to save a great deal of money. How?

It comes back to cost of use—because the cost of living in a particular house is far greater than the cost of the house.

There are utilities, insurance, taxes, etc. that typically increase in direct proportion to the dollar value of the house. There are also less obvious costs—call them social costs—such as what sort of car you drive, what sort of furniture you buy, whether you send your kids to private school and, if so, what schools you choose. These costs can be huge, yet most people do not consider them when thinking about "moving up" as their income rises.

Most people take for granted that a more expensive home will provide for more dollar appreciation and, therefore, is a better investment. But when your social costs are tens or hundreds of thousands of extra dollars per year, that may not be so.

I am not saying that you should be happy with your starter house. But I am saying that once you are established in a home that you love, you should keep it as long as you possibly can. When you get the raise, don't run out and buy another house that is $100,000 more expensive.

Instead, figure out what you can do to your present home to make it more enjoyable. Even though the $20,000 you may spend renovating the kitchen is not money you'd get back later if you sold, the pleasure it will give you—in terms of a rich life—could be enormous.

Meanwhile, the extra $100,000 you spend on a bigger house could easily cost you more than $1 million in social costs over twenty years.

I know this is a difficult concept to grasp. It flies in the face of conventional wisdom. But the fact is that you will spend less money in the long run by having the nicest house in your old neighborhood than you will by buying up and expecting big gains in property appreciation.

I give myself as an example. I have owned and lived in three houses in South Florida in the last thirty years. I lived in the first one for three years, the second for seven, and the current one for close to twenty years. I could have easily bought a more expensive home years ago. But I didn't. My home was both big enough and small enough (see above) to meet my needs.

I've put good money into redoing my home over that time. In fact, there is almost never a year when I don't make some improvement. But the money I spend is nothing compared with the money I'd have wasted if I had foolishly bought up.

Home Ownership as an Investment

The World War II generation got lucky with their starter homes. Although they "moved up" once or twice, most of them settled for at least a dozen years while their children were in school. And they had the benefit of the enormous price appreciation of property that took place during the 1960s and 1970s.

When they became empty nesters in the late '70s and early '80s, they were able to sell their larger homes for many times what they originally paid for them. By moving into smaller homes, they were able to put a good portion of those profits into accounts that funded their retirements.

As children of that generation, baby boomers mistakenly assumed that they would be able to do the same thing. It seemed axiomatic that house prices would always go up—significantly, if you were willing to give it some time.

This myth was one of the reasons millions of Americans lost trillions of dollars when the real estate bubble burst in 2007-2008. Even after property values had escalated beyond reason, people believed they would continue to rise. So they felt confident taking second and third mortgages that eventually wiped them out.

We know better now. History tells us that on a long-term, nationwide basis, property values rise at or just above (1 or 2 percent) the rate of inflation. That is a good thing in that property can protect the investor against inflation—a terrible wealth destroyer. But if you are looking at real estate strictly from the perspective of appreciation, this average return on investment is far from spectacular.

In terms of quality of life, though—which is what we're talking about here—you don't want to think of your house the same way you might think of your stocks or bonds. It's okay if the money you put into it doesn't earn you 8 or 12 percent on a yearly basis.

My view is that so long as I can get the money I put into my house out of it, adjusted for inflation, I'm happy. And you can do that if you make smart spending decisions.

Shopping for Your Perfect Home

When shopping for a home, think first about location. Try to pinpoint the type of community that best matches your sense of living well. Some people would like a quiet suburb. Others would prefer an urban setting with access to theaters and museums. Still others would want to live near a beach or in the mountains.

Even if you feel that you are "stuck" working for a company that is located in a particular place, determining your ideal community will be a very useful exercise. Because in doing so, you will be discovering your core values, values that will help you make all of the important "living rich" decisions you will face in your life.

Also keep in mind that companies are relocating like never before. And in the Internet Age, telecommuting is becoming more and more common. So you may not be as "stuck" as you think you are.

Buying a house is a huge decision. You have to get the money part right. But you also have to get the neighborhood right. For one thing, you have to consider the social and recreational needs of your entire family. And that can be complicated. If you have young children, will they be able to walk to school with their friends? Will they have easy access to sports programs? Who will your close neighbors be—and will you have much in common with them?

There are practical considerations as well—zoning laws, neighborhood covenants, and property taxes, for example.

You have to spend time investigating all of these things before you start the actual house hunt. Then, once you have found an optimal neighborhood, you can have the fun of wandering around and looking at houses.

A house is a complicated thing. Its structure will affect the quality of your life in a dozen ways. So you should have a good idea of what you are looking for.

How many bedrooms and bathrooms? How large a kitchen, dining room, and living room? Will a one-car garage suffice or do you need three bays? Do you need a writing or sculpture studio? A basement or attic? What about a vegetable garden?

Does it have to be new (or fairly new), or would you be willing to deal with the eccentricities of an older house? Even if the previous owners kept it in good shape, the infrastructure of older homes tends to need ongoing attention. And you'll probably need to budget more for utilities, since the home's envelope won't be as tight as with newer construction and older furnaces, hot water heaters, and cooling systems aren't as efficient.

Maybe you will find exactly what you are looking for in the right neighborhood at the right price. More likely, you will have to make compromises.

By thinking of your home as a haven ("Someone interesting lives here!") and not a status symbol ("Someone rich lives here!") or an investment, you can spend a reasonable amount of money on it each year, making it increasingly "richer."

Your goal is always to enhance your pleasure, utility, or comfort. And in my experience, even small things can make a big difference. Resist the urge to make everything bigger or newer. Bigger and newer, as you remember, are the values of the poor-minded person. You are thinking rich.

Chapter 3

The Rich Man's Home: Making It Ever Richer and More Perfect

A rich house is one in which every room (and every space within every room) serves a useful purpose and provides some related pleasure.

Most homeowners understand this in regard to the kitchen. The kitchen typically has several important functions: the preparation and cooking of meals... the storage of food and dishes and cooking paraphernalia... and sometimes as a place for the family to congregate. Thus, the kitchen is one of the most important rooms in the house. The rich kitchen achieves the twin goals of purposefulness and pleasure neatly. It is, therefore, no larger or more elaborate than it needs to be. It contains no more fixtures or amenities than the family needs. The ambiance is friendly and casual. The arrangement of appliances and surfaces optimizes efficiency. Storage is logical. The eating space, if there is one, feels comfortable.

This idea of purposefulness and pleasure is difficult for some people to grasp. They can understand the value of having an inviting and functional kitchen, but they also see the kitchen as a symbol of success. Thus we have the gargantuan refrigerators, "professional" stoves, diner-sized counters, cookbook libraries, and an overall volume that would be appropriate for a mid-sized restaurant rather than a mid-sized family.

When K and I redesigned our kitchen, we came very close to falling into that trap. Many of our neighbors had bought into the "bigger is better" craziness and, at the time, it seemed like the thing to do. Fortunately, we came to our senses. We reminded ourselves of how uncomfortable we felt when we were in those oversized kitchens, and we certainly didn't want our guests to feel the same way. We looked at each other and rolled our eyes. And we promised ourselves that it wouldn't happen in our house... to us or to our guests.

To make sure that our kitchen would be both purposeful and pleasurable, we made it large enough to accommodate two cooks working at the same time and a table for eight, but no larger than that. And because we wanted it to feel cozy too, we added lots of indirect and accent lighting to give the room atmosphere when we ate there.

We installed a central counter around which people could gather, a gas-burning stove (for K) and a hidden microwave (for me), a spigot over the range for filling pasta pots with water, and a hidden blender that pops up when you open one of the cabinet doors. All of it very purposeful.

Then, to make our kitchen interesting and aesthetically appealing, we installed display cabinets for some of the glass sculptures that we collect. And we covered the walls, like all the walls in our house, with art.

The "purposeful and pleasing" standard applies to every room of your house. If you have an "entertainment room," for example, it should be space that makes it easy for you, your family, and guests to get together, converse, and have fun. If you have a dining room, it should be conducive to dining—and not just once or twice a year but often.

Dens and libraries should be quiet retreats. Bathrooms should be mini-sanctuaries. Living rooms should be places where living takes place, not dress-up rooms that nobody ever uses.

And it's not just every room. It's every space. Every part of the kitchen and the living room and the bedroom. And all the spaces in between. Every space should serve a purpose and provide pleasure. Nothing should be there for show. Every chair or sofa should want to be sat upon. Every table sat at. Every appliance used.

If your house does not measure up right now, there is a a lot that you can do to make it "richer" over time without spending a ton of money.

Home Improvement the "Living Rich" Way

A fresh coat of paint can turn an otherwise dreary room into a cheery one.

You can make a kitchen look new and bright by replacing countertops and/or cabinets. There are many surprisingly good options available at stores like Home Depot. The installation is not that complicated. You can do it yourself or use someone recommended by the store or by someone you know.

Furniture can make a big difference, and you don't have to buy it new. Browsing secondhand furniture stores and consignment shops is a great way to spend a rainy Saturday. Piece by piece, you can refresh and/or reinvent every room on a budget.

An often overlooked element in the feel of a house is light. Spaces—inside and out—can be miraculously transformed by adding, subtracting, or altering the light. If you have a sense of what lighting can do, you will be able to make major changes by introducing indirect or natural lighting and/or repositioning fixtures. If you don't feel like you can do this on your own, hire a lighting expert to spend a few hours with you. Even at $100 an hour, you will get your money's worth.

As with other aspects of living rich, making your house richer is a matter of spending your dollars wisely. That means buying expertise when you don't have it, but it also means learning from experts so that you can gradually develop skills of your own.

Rather than hiring a designer or decorator to "redo" your entire house, bring in someone to work with you on a single small project—maybe a bathroom or bedroom. The process will help you learn what you like and what options are available so that you can try to do the next room on your own.

You can also learn a great deal by paging through magazines and home-improvement books. But keep in mind that you are looking for ideas that will meet your objectives. Don't be seduced by photos of rooms that shout, "Someone rich owns me." Look for small things that will enhance your family's ability to use and enjoy the home.

And the Internet, of course, is loaded with useful resources. Pinterest.com and Houzz.com have thousands of images that you can use for ideas on products, decor, and room renovation. Members can get their questions answered by the people who posted the photos, many of whom are professionals. Sherwin-Williams and Benjamin Moore have online applications that let you upload photos and "paint" walls, trim, windows, and doors.

I've used these online applications, and they are really helpful. You can see how your house (inside or out) will look with all sorts of different color combinations. You don't have to buy quarts of sample colors and test them on the house the way you had to do when I was younger.

The Major Renovation

If you are doing a major renovation—a completely new kitchen, wing, guesthouse, etc.—you are going to have to hire an architect and a contractor and go through the permit process.

Architects are there to help you make the big decisions: the look, the feel, the size, and the purpose of the renovation. They also create loads of very precise blueprints for your contractor and subcontractors.

A good architect is a great ally in living rich. A bad architect or a bad relationship with a good architect will make you emotionally and financially poorer.

An architect's fee can be structured as a fixed amount, an hourly rate, or a percentage of the construction cost (usually 10 percent). In my experience, a fixed amount is best because it gives the architect the incentive to keep the job simple.

To get the best value from an architect, it helps to have a very good idea of what you want before you begin. If you come prepared with sample floor plans and photographs, the entire process will be faster, easier, and less expensive. Plus you will be assured of getting something you really like.

The right design will start your renovation on the right path. A competent and experienced contractor will keep it moving in the desired direction.

Most architects have relationships with contractors and will recommend one for your project. But a contractor who has been recommended by a friend or colleague might be even a better choice. Even if you think you know that you want a particular contractor, it's a good idea to check out several possibilities. Not only to make sure that you're getting a good price, but also to guarantee that you're getting a contractor who will do a good job for you.

You can learn a lot about how a contractor operates from how organized his work site is, as well as by how many hours he is actually there and who manages the work when he isn't. Ask how he hires his subs, how long he's worked with them, and how he finds backups when someone can't make it to the job. Ask how he handles cost overruns and how he will keep you informed about progress or problems. And there will be problems. When they arise, you should expect your contractor to advise you of available options and guide you toward appropriate choices.

Home Improvement Dollars and Sense

Ignore the advice of the "experts" that tell you to make only those improvements that will give you back, in sales value, a dollar for every dollar that you spend. Very few upgrades or remodeling projects recoup 100 percent of their cost. According to *Remodeling* magazine, on average, you can expect to get back $57 for every $100 you spend.

But that ratio is based on the assumption that you would be selling the home shortly thereafter. And from a living rich perspective, that's not what you're going to do. You're going to find a good house in the right neighborhood at the right price. And you're going to plan to keep that house for ten or twenty (or more) years—making it richer and more perfect every year. So for you, such ratios are meaningless.

Still, you have to have a way to quantify the expense. And as with every other decision you're going to make about spending your money to live rich, your guiding rule should be cost of use. (See Chapter 2.) Rather than worry about whether you can get a 50 or 90 percent return on a particular improvement in a single year, you figure out how much it will be on a cost of use basis.

Let's look at a rough example. You want to update your kitchen. The estimate is $10,000. Your guess is that it will increase the value of your home by $6,000 (a 60 percent return). So you do the calculation. The additional cost of use will be $4,000 divided by ten years or $400 a year. That comes to about $33 a month or a dollar a day.

Then you can ask yourself: Will this remodeling job give me at least a dollar a day in additional pleasure? Putting it that way makes the answer obvious.

Chapter 4

The Rich Man's Bed

Of the many material objects that affect the quality of your life, there are few more important than the bed you sleep in.

In terms of time spent, it may occupy the first position. After all, if you are like most people, you spend a third of your life in bed.

Unless you have slept in a really good bed, you may not realize what a difference it makes. I spent the first forty-something years of my life sleeping on cheap beds. Back then, I thought that tossing and turning all night was normal.

About twenty years ago, K and I spent a few nights in The Benjamin, an expensive midtown Manhattan hotel. The bed we slept on was distinctly better than ours at home. Slipping into bed felt luxurious because of the silky linens. Lying in bed felt more comfortable. No lumps. No hollows. The mattress was soft but firm. We slept like babies.

I studied the bed in the morning. The frame was nothing special. But the box spring and the mattress looked considerably more solid than ours. And the linens were obviously of a high quality.

We asked the concierge if he happened to know what kind of bedding the hotel used. Not only did he know, he handed me a brochure about it. Apparently, we weren't the only guests who'd asked.

This was actually the beginning of a trend in "super beds" that luxury hotels were getting into at the time. Today, you can buy the mattresses and linens you sleep on from many hotels all over the world.

For me, it was a revelation. I had never before given a second thought to bedding. I had never imagined that I was sleeping like a pauper—that by buying a better bed I could sleep like a billionaire.

When we got home, K ordered the same mattress and linens we had fallen in love with at The Benjamin. They were expensive—much more than we would have considered spending before then. They arrived several weeks later, and we were not disappointed. K has replaced the linens periodically, but that mattress (and box spring) kept us comfortable for nearly twenty years.

About a year ago, the mattress felt like it was losing support at the sides. It was still relatively comfortable, but it was time to buy a new one. Before we did, we went online and looked at our options. And they were overwhelming. In the span of twenty years, the marketplace for mattresses had expanded more than tenfold.

Since I was already scribbling notes for this book, I asked my colleagues at *The Palm Beach Letter* to have their research team do a serious review of mattresses for me. I asked them to identify the major types, explain the plusses and minuses of each, and then analyze the data.

When I looked at their findings (hundreds of pages!), one thing was clear. With beds, as with other material objects, the old saw that you get what you pay for is only partially true. In some cases, quality costs more. In other cases, it doesn't.

We found, for example, one mattress that sells for $60,000 and half a dozen in the $15,000 to $25,000 range. We tried several of them out. They felt great and had impressive stories attached to them. But were they better than the best $1,000 mattresses?

Read on to find out.

The Search for the Perfect Mattress

Let's begin, as we should in discussing any *thing* we will be discussing in the book, with a definition of quality. When it comes to mattresses, quality means comfort, support, and durability.

Your mattress has to be comfortable. It must give you that "I'm in heaven" feeling when you stretch out on it. It also has to be engineered to give you proper spinal support so that you wake up feeling like a million dollars. And, finally, it has to be durable. It must be made to last—without losing its support— for at least ten years.

Support and durability are things that can be measured and recorded. But comfort cannot. It is therefore impossible to create a definitive ranking of mattresses in terms of quality. But we can explain the features of each kind of mattress, emphasizing the benefits and drawbacks of each. And we can report the reported impressions of people in terms of comfort.

The Innerspring—the Most Popular Mattress

An innerspring mattress is made up of steel coils padded with layers of padding for insulation and cushioning. The outermost layer—the one you see—is often quilted and can be made of anything from damask (the highest quality) to cotton, cotton/poly blend, or vinyl. And the whole thing sits atop a box spring or platform.

Here's what you need to know when looking at innerspring mattresses:

• **The Coil Count**

The job of the coils is to distribute the weight of the body. The more coils a mattress has, the firmer it will be. The softest innersprings have roughly 250 coils. The firmest have as many as 1,000.

• **The Gauge of the Steel**

The gauge (thickness) of the steel wire in the coils is another factor. The lower the gauge, the thicker the wire. A mattress with 300 coils of 12-gauge wire will be firmer than a mattress with 300 coils of 14-gauge wire.

How firm should your mattress be?

Consider the mattress you have now. If you can't roll over easily, the mattress is probably too soft for you. If you feel excess pressure on your hips and shoulders, it is probably too firm. Lie on your back and see if you can slide your hand under the small of your back. If there is enough of a gap that your hand slides in easily, you should look for a softer mattress.

• The Arrangement of the Coils

The coils can either interlock or be independent. If they interlock, they are tied together with wire. If they are independent, each individual coil is "pocketed" in cloth. Pocketed coil mattresses require more coils because each one must work on its own to support you. As a result, they give you better contouring and reduce the amount of flex in the mattress when your partner moves during the night.

• The Padding

Over the years, the coils have not really changed. But manufacturers have added more padding, anywhere from three to eight layers. You may be surprised to know that it's worn-out padding, not broken-down coils, that causes sagging in a mattress. And the padding determines a large part of the cost of a mattress.

The way manufacturers stitch the padding together is just as important as the quality of the material in it. In better mattresses, each layer is stitched in place by hand. This keeps the layers from shifting and creating lumps.

• The "Pillow Top" Option

A "pillow top" adds a layer of softness to a firm mattress, but it also adds to the cost. And it can go flat long before the mattress itself wears out.

If you like the feel of a pillow top, you might be better off purchasing a separate mattress topper. They are available in memory foam (probably your best choice in terms of comfort and durability), sheepskin (which is warm in the winter and cool in the summer), and as featherbeds (which give you the simple pleasure of sinking down into something incredibly soft).

• **Edge Support**

Innerspring mattresses tend to break down around the edges first. A mattress with heavier-gauge coils and thicker padding around the edges will help it hold its shape.

Benefits of the Innerspring Mattress

- It's available in a wide range of prices and with many optional features.

- Some models can be flipped to prolong the life of the mattress.

- When you move or turn over, very little of that motion is transferred to the other side of the bed, which makes pocket-coil innersprings well-suited for couples.

Drawbacks of the Innerspring Mattress

- It's difficult to comparison shop.

- The innerspring is less durable than the other mattress types, so it has to be replaced more frequently.

- Most require the purchase of a box spring, which has to be replaced whenever you replace the mattress.

Keep in Mind: Over the last ten years, there have been significant improvements in mattress construction. As long as you stay away from the low end of the market (less than $800 for a queen mattress), durability should be consistent across most brands and models. A top-of-the-line innerspring will have pocketed coils and a top layer of memory foam. Many manufacturers now offer this option.

To Space and Back:
The Memory Foam Mattress

The origin of the memory foam mattress goes back to the 1970s when scientists developed a viscoelastic material for NASA. It was used as cushioning and support for astronauts during liftoff. It was pressure sensitive and molded quickly to the shape of a body pressing into it. And because it was temperature sensitive, they called it "temper foam."

In the 1980s, the material was perfected to be used in mattresses. The first memory foam mattresses were produced for hospitals. But feedback from patients—which included claims of better sleep and less back pain—led to widespread commercial interest. People especially liked the pleasant feeling of "melting" into it.

The Tempur-Pedic brand is the gold standard. It uses the original formula for the foam, but in recent years other companies have copied it.

Whether you buy Tempur-Pedic or one of the generics, the key things to consider in a memory foam mattress are thickness and density.

• **Thickness**

A thicker mattress does not necessarily mean it has more memory foam. A 13-inch mattress could have anywhere from three to five inches of memory foam. The rest could be made up of foam that has less "give."

• **Density**

The lower the density of the memory foam, the lower the price. As the density increases, so does the amount of support it gives you. Anything less than three pounds per cubic foot is considered low grade. High-quality foam is at least five pounds per cubic foot. You need enough density to support your body. But if you get too much for your body weight, the mattress won't give you that pleasant melting feeling.

Benefits of Memory Foam

- It's antibacterial and allergen and dust mite resistant.

- Like the pocket-coil innerspring, very little motion is transferred to your partner's side of the bed when you move or turn over.

- It conforms to the body in response to heat and pressure and returns to its original shape.

- It is extremely durable. (Most memory foam mattresses have a twenty-year warranty.)

Drawbacks of Memory Foam

- Some people say that memory foam makes them feel like they are sinking into quicksand.

- Others complain that it traps body heat and makes them uncomfortably hot.

- It tends to be much more expensive than the traditional innerspring mattress.

- Some memory foam mattresses have an odd chemical smell that can be irritating to the nose or throat.

Keep in Mind: Some generic memory foam is less resilient and less durable than the memory foam with the Tempur-Pedic name. And there is some generic memory foam that eventually starts to turn into sharp-edged gel beads. But that doesn't mean you have to buy the high-priced Tempur-pedic brand. There are manufacturers of memory foam that is every bit as good… and significantly less expensive.

Latex Foam—the Latest in Sleep Comfort

Latex foam mattresses can be made of 100 percent natural latex (collected from rubber trees), 100 percent synthetic latex (a blend of petrochemicals), or a combination of the two.

Both natural and synthetic latex foam is similar to memory foam in many important ways. It minimizes pressure on the body, especially the neck and back. It is antimicrobial and antibacterial. Dust mites can't live in it, and it is extremely durable. In fact, pure latex mattresses are by far the most durable that you can buy. They are also the most expensive.

• **Dunlop vs. Talalay**

Both natural and synthetic latex foam can be produced in two ways: by the Dunlop method or by the Talalay method. The Dunlop method produces latex with a somewhat firmer, more buoyant feel. The Talalay method is newer and is used primarily for synthetic latex. It produces a softer, less firm mattress. Some latex mattresses have a combination of both Dunlop and Talalay latex. Neither type is superior. What you choose is a matter of personal preference.

• **Customizing the Layers**

A mattress can be manufactured with one, two, three, or four layers of 3-inch latex foam. And you can customize the firmness of each layer (soft, medium, or firm). You might, for example, go with Dunlop latex on the bottom and Talalay on the top. This would give you a foundation layer with good support and a top layer with a luxurious feel. You can also choose a different level of firmness for each side of the mattress.

• The "Hybrid" Mattress

It is not feasible for any mattress under $1,500 to be 100 percent latex foam. Some manufacturers will label a mattress as 100 percent when, in fact, there are only one or two inches of latex in the entire thing.

Other manufacturers, in an effort to take advantage of the marketing cachet of latex foam, have come up with the idea of the "hybrid" mattress. They might, for example, top the coils of an innerspring mattress with a layer of latex foam or wrap the individual coils with it. (They do this with memory foam too.)

This does keep the cost of the mattress down, but know what you're getting. If what you want is a latex foam mattress, make sure it has a latex core.

Benefits of Latex Foam

- It's breathable and resilient.

- It eliminates motion transfers.

- It's supportive, conforms to the body, and relieves pressure points.

- It's antibacterial and resistant to dust mites, mold, mildew, and other allergens.

- It's the longest-lasting mattress type on the market—some say thirty years.

Drawbacks of Latex Foam

- It's fairly new on the market, so it's not widely available. You may not be able to test it before you buy, and you may have to buy it online.

- It does not have as many features/options as innerspring or memory foam.

- Like memory foam, it tends to feel warm—but not as warm.

- It's very expensive.

Keep in Mind: Organic latex foam is 100 percent natural and chemical-free. The rubber tree is a renewable resource, so the foam is eco-friendly and biodegradable. If this is important to you, be aware that in a mattress labeled "100 percent latex," some or all of it may be synthetic. Instead, look for a mattress labeled "100 percent *natural* latex."

The Adjustable Airbed— Putting You in Control

You can get a simple air mattress to put on the floor when company comes—or a luxurious airbed for yourself, with multiple air chambers, extensive padding, a sturdy frame, and even remote controls. With these beds, each person can independently adjust the level of firmness on their side of the mattress by pumping more or less air into it.

The "Sleep Number" bed, manufactured by the Select Comfort company, is the one you're probably familiar with.

• **The Air Chambers**

The ideal thickness of an air bladder should be five to seven inches. This is meaty enough to support larger folks without bottoming out, especially at softer settings.

• The Pump System

The pump should be accessible, not buried inside the airbed. It should be able to move a lot of air very quickly—to fill the bed in less than two minutes, from dead empty. And it should be *quiet*.

• The Controls

You will have the choice of wired or wireless remote controls to adjust the firmness of your bed. Wireless is convenient, but the remotes can get lost easily.

• Edge Support

Stay away from airbeds with air chambers that go all the way to the edge. Thick, sturdy foam side rails should be part of the airbed design.

Benefits of the Airbed

- The firmness of the bed can be adjusted to suit your specific preference.

- Each side of the bed can be independently adjusted.

- Quality brands offer many features, including the option of memory foam comfort layers.

Drawbacks of the Airbed

- It usually comes in pieces (six to ten of them) and has to be assembled.

- It has a lot of components that can require repair or replacement. Air chambers wear out over time, and the source of a leak may be hard to find.

- You probably will not be able to try it out before you buy it.

Keep in Mind: Since you won't know if you like an airbed until you sleep on it, a good warranty is a must. Return policies can vary from retailer to retailer, even on the same model. Study the warranty before you make a purchase.

Shopping for Sheets

The comfort and durability of sheets depends on the fabric, thread count, and weave.

• The Fabric

Most high-quality sheets are made of cotton, with Egyptian cotton considered the most luxurious. Sea Island cotton has long fibers that make it feel like silk, but it is in short supply. (It grows only in the West Indies, parts of Georgia, and the Carolinas.) This makes it a very expensive choice for bedding. Pima cotton, developed from Egyptian cotton by farmers in the Southwestern U.S., is known for its softness and durability. Bamboo-cotton blend sheets are soft, breathable, and easy to care for. Another plant fiber that is often blended with cotton is Modal.

• The Thread Count

Thread count is the number of threads per square inch of fabric. The threads can be single-ply or two-ply (two strands twisted together). Two-ply threads are stronger, but they are also stiffer.

A thread count between 300 and 400 is the sweet spot for comfort and durability. Sheets in that range will be smooth, soft, absorbent, and breathable. Don't be fooled into thinking you need sheets with a super-high thread count. That's often just an excuse for manufacturers to charge more. And, in fact, *Consumer Reports* found that some manufacturers claiming 800-1,200 thread counts were using creative math. When they analyzed 1,200-thread-count sheets in the lab, many of them turned out to be a little above 400.

• **The Weave**

The weave of the fabric affects how the sheet feels. Percale is closely woven with a fine texture. It feels crisp and luxurious while also being durable. Sateen has a softer, more luxurious feel and a glossier look, but is not as durable as percale. It also has a tendency to snag. Twill is a heavier weave that stands up well and is less likely to wrinkle.

Shopping for Pillows

The general rule is to replace your pillows every twelve to eighteen months, and definitely after two years. If you fold a pillow in half and it does not unfold—at least partially—on its own, it is time for a new one.

Firm, Medium, or Soft?

If you sleep on your side, you'll be most comfortable with a firm pillow that cradles your neck. If you sleep on your back, a medium to firm pillow will help support the natural curve of your spine. And if you're a stomach sleeper, a soft, thin pillow will ease the strain of your neck being turned to the side.

Natural or Synthetic Fill?

Polyester is inexpensive, hypoallergenic, and machine washable. A poly-cluster pillow (polyester clusters covered with silicone) can feel much like down, without the high cost. Note: Polyester pillows can be especially attractive to dust mites.

Memory foam and latex foam are hypoallergenic and give you excellent neck support. They hold their shape longer than polyester, so you will not have to replace them as often. The foam pillows do tend to feel warm, though. And you might notice a slight odor, but it will soon fade.

Natural feather and down pillows are extremely comfortable. They are more expensive than polyester or foam, but they also last longer. Though they can trigger allergies in some people, it is possible to find feather/down pillows that are hypo-allergenic.

How Much Do You Have to Spend?

You can buy a polyester pillow for as little as $5. The foam, feather, and down pillows can set you back as much as $100. But spending more does not necessarily buy you a better pillow. For example, *Consumer Reports* found that a cheaper version of the memory foam pillow scored just as well as a higher-priced version… and it was $60 cheaper.

As with mattresses, the important thing is how it feels to you.

You've Decided on a Mattress… Now You Have to Buy It

The first thing you see when you walk into a mattress store is row after row of mattresses. At first, they all look the same. The second thing you see is the sales associate approaching you.

Here's where you go from there…

• **Don't waste your time with a trainee.**

Make sure you're talking to someone with lots of experience— someone familiar with all the mattresses in the store.

• Ask about their return policy.

This might sound like a strange thing to start out with—but if you don't like their return policy, there's no reason to shop there. Store policies can range from "final sale" to "thirty days" and even "unlimited returns."

• Compare apples to apples.

Manufacturers change the names of identical mattresses for different retailers. One store's "super plush" could be another store's "super soft." So if you go by name alone, you will think you are looking at two different mattresses.

It's just marketing talk. As long as you know the features you want, you will be able to make an informed decision.

• The fifteen-minute test

When you find a mattress that interests you, test it by lying down on it in your normal sleep position. To get a good feel for the mattress, give it a minimum of fifteen minutes.

• Ask about the manufacturer's warranty.

A warranty can help protect you against defects in workmanship. But it will not protect you against normal wear and tear. And it is NOT a guarantee of durability or comfort. Most warrantees are for ten or twenty years. But do not assume that the length of the warranty has any connection with how long your mattress will be comfortable.

• Never pay retail!

You can often get an excellent price on a mattress by buying it online. If you have already shopped in person… have given several mattresses the fifteen-minute test… and know exactly what you want… you can buy a mattress online with a fair degree of confidence.

But you can get a great deal at a brick-and-mortar store too. Markups on mattresses are enormous. Some of the best-known brands can be marked up by as much as 500 percent! This gives you a lot of room for negotiating, and it's well worth doing. Most mattress retailers, including some department stores, allow their salespeople to negotiate. And according to *Consumer Reports*, 72 percent of those who do a bit of haggling get a lower price.

Chapter 5

The Rich Man's Car

You think it might be time to buy a new car. The thought begins tentatively and then sprouts roots. You do some research. You talk to some friends. The more you think about it, the better you like the idea. Pretty soon, you are itching to do it… and you find yourself in a showroom.

A "sales associate" approaches. A friendly guy, he asks what you are looking for. If you don't know, he asks about your driving needs. He may ask where you live, the size of your family, etc.

If he sees that you have a fondness for a particular model, he gets more animated. But if you change your mind, he doesn't push you. He's ready to sell you the car you want to buy.

There is one car on the floor—the most expensive one there—that retails for more than $100,000. "That's a car for billionaires," you think. "It's not for me." You don't want to endure the pain of envy, so you avoid looking at it. Instead, you look at sedans in the $25,000-$40,000 range.

You settle for a sensible $30,000 sedan—one very much like the sensible sedan you've been driving. You tell the salesman that this is the car you want, but you can't pay more than X number of dollars per month for it. He says, "I don't know if I can do that, but I'll try."

He disappears into the back office. Five minutes later, he returns with an offer. It is much higher than what you said you could pay. You object. You haggle over the trade-in value of your car and he disappears into the back office and comes back again. The monthly payment is still $45 too high. You haggle some more and he makes another trip to the back office "on your behalf." Coming back with a smile on his face, he tells you that he thinks he can come really close to your number if you come up with a slightly higher down payment. You reluctantly agree.

The final number is still $20 more than what you wanted, but it's okay. You can afford it.

Next, he introduces you to a nicely dressed woman who is the dealer's finance manager. She asks you many questions and has you fill out many forms. At the end of the process, you realize that you are paying an additional $25 more per month because of extra warranties, treatments, etc. that she makes you feel you should have known about.

You are committed emotionally to having the car. So you sign the papers, feeling a little bit had.

The salesman shows you the ropes with your new car—how to adjust the side reflectors and jack up the radio. It's pretty exciting. You leave an hour later, happy, with that new car aroma in your nose.

All is good.

A few weeks later, the new car smell is gone. After a month or two, there is a little scratch on the passenger door. It is still a nice car, and you still like it. But it is no longer a new car. It's a used car.

Four or five years later, you repeat the process. You never stop to realize that for the same money you have been spending on your so-so $30,000 sedans, you could have been driving that amazing $100,000 machine.

A Much Smarter Approach

I own two cars: a 12-cylinder 2007 BMW 760Li and a 1991 Acura NSX. The BMW is a sedan. The NSX is a high-performance sports car. Both are exceptional vehicles. They look great. They drive great. And people perceive them as world-class automobiles.

To buy these two cars new today, you'd have to fork over more than $250,000. But that would be foolish. You can drive luxury cars like these for a tiny fraction of what you'd expect.

Most people, when considering the cost of an automobile, think only in terms of the monthly payment. "I don't care about the price of the car," they say. "All I care about is how much I have to pay every month."

This, they think, is smart, bottom-line thinking. But it is exactly the worst kind of thinking when it comes to buying cars because it puts the car salesperson in charge of what kind of car you will ultimately buy. When he hears your number, he will think he will be able to get you to spend 10 to 15 percent more and he will put you in a car that will give him the best commission.

In other words, when you tell a car salesman that you can't pay more than X number of dollars per month, you are pretty much saying, "I am a financial dummy. Do unto me as you wish."

Let's Talk About My Cars

I bought my NSX when it first came out. At the time, it was the state-of-the-art high-performance sports car. Honda had invested hundreds of millions of dollars in its design. There was not another sports car in the world that could equal it in terms of performance, quality, and reliability.

I paid $70,000 for it. That's a lot of money—more money than you probably believe you can afford. But the fact is my NSX is the cheapest car I've ever owned.

If I were to sell it today, twenty-three years later, I could easily get $35,000. And because it is a Honda (and not a Ferrari or a Porsche), the cost of repairs and maintenance has been very low. I have spent no more than $5,000 on it since I bought it.

That means my "cost of use"—the concept I introduced you to in Chapter 2—has been about $150 per month.

Here's the math: initial purchase price ($70,000) plus $5,000 in repairs and maintenance minus its current resale value ($35,000— it's in mint condition) gives me $40,000 divided by 276 months (23 years): a little less than $145.

Even if I had financed the car instead of paying cash, it would have been a bargain. What made it a bargain? Not the $70,000 sticker price. That was, as I said, a ton of money back then. What has made my purchase a great deal is the fact that I have kept that car for twenty-three years. I would have had an even better deal had I been able to buy it a year or so later at a discount. With the NSXs, this wasn't possible. But with most luxury cars, it is.

My 12-cylinder 2007 BMW 760Li is an equally wonderful car. It is big, comfortable, drives like a dream, and has immense power and all sorts of fancy amenities (including a refrigerator for champagne).

If you had bought it new in 2007 (with the added features I have), you would have paid about $120,000. But as a person who knows how to live rich, you would have bought it in 2009 or 2010 with 20,000 or 30,000 miles on the odometer for $70,000.

That number may surprise you. Is it possible to buy a low-mileage, two- or three-year-old luxury car for 60 to 70 percent of its new price?

The answer is yes, for two reasons:

- The more expensive the car, the greater the depreciation rate in its early years.

- Extras such as the low-profile rims and tires I bought are worth close to nothing on resales, which benefits the secondhand buyer.

And if you enjoy your 760Li for twenty years (as I expect to enjoy mine), it will end up costing you a lot less than the five or six mediocre cars you would otherwise be driving in that time.

The Living Rich Car-Buying Strategy in a Nutshell

I can't tell you exactly which car to buy. But I can help you make the right decision. To make my strategy work for you, there are four main factors to consider.

- The car you buy

- The price you pay for it

- The price you can sell it for

- How long you will keep it

The Car You Buy

To drive like a billionaire, you must drive an exceptional car. By exceptional I mean a car that is beautiful, comfortable, functional, and durable. It should also be a car that makes you feel rich. Often, this means buying an expensive car. But that, as we've learned, is not the most important factor in the equation.

The Price You Pay for It

The best way to save money on any car is to buy it used.

Here's the thing…

The instant you drive a new car off the lot, it loses value. According to research that my colleagues at *The Palm Beach Letter* did for me, the market value of a brand-new $20,000 car instantly drops to only $17,800 when you drive it home from the dealer. By years three or four, that same car will have lost 50 percent of its value. And after five years, it's worth about only 37 percent of its original cost.

To me, the "sweet spot" is when the car has depreciated by about 40 to 50 percent but is still in great condition. With most cars, this means three to five years old and with 50,000 or fewer miles on it.

The second best way to save money on your car is to pay cash for it. New cars sometimes come with great financing packages. The cost of the loan is cheap, but you are still paying too much for the car. And when you buy a used car, the financing can be expensive. A $25,000 loan financed at 6.9 percent for two years will end up costing you almost $3,500 in interest charges.

The Price You Can Sell It For

As I said, all cars depreciate a great deal in the first few years. But what's nice about luxury cars is that they tend to depreciate less. In other words, they hold their value better.

This is not true of all luxury cars, but it is true for most of the best of them. My NSX, for example, lost about half of its value after four years but then did not depreciate at all after that. Now, more than twenty years later, I can still sell it for half of what I paid for it. That's because not many of these cars were produced, and the one I have is in near-perfect condition.

How Long You Keep It

It all comes down to "cost of use." And the most important factor in determining the cost of use of a car is the number of years you intend to keep it. The longer you drive it, the more bang you get for your buck.

And thus we get back to one of the most important rules about living rich: Buy quality and keep it for a long time.

When it comes to cars, that means buying the best models of the best brands... buying them when they are two to five years old and then keeping them for ten to twenty years.

You may be thinking, "Oh, I would never want to own a car that long. It would soon be out of date."

But this won't happen if you are smart and buy the best cars from the best car manufacturers. Cars that are classically beautiful, designed for comfort, capable of high performance, and built to last.

The NSX that I bought when it first came out is cooler now than it was then. The new sports cars may be a bit faster. And they may have some options that my car doesn't have. But you can't drive a car faster than my NSX legally (except on a racetrack). And those extra options? The "cool factor" of having a vintage NSX outranks them by a mile.

The same will be true of my BMW. I chose it because of its classic styling. It will look great in ten years and in twenty years, just as a vintage 1980 or 1990 BMW looks great today.

What's Your Dream Car?

There's probably a car you've always lusted after—the car you tell yourself you'll buy as soon as you're financially able. Well... now you are.

Chapter 6

The Rich Man's Meal

Food is undoubtedly one of the great pleasures in life. But it can also be a significant danger. If you aren't careful about what you eat, you can easily become overweight, fatigued, and sick.

Wealthy people, as a group, tend to eat better than their less-wealthy counterparts. Studies show that they know more about food, are more discriminating in their purchases, and spend more time enjoying their meals. And the richest of the rich—billionaires— have a life expectancy that's three-and-a-half years longer than that of the average person, according to *Forbes* magazine.

Rich people don't have to think about price. They can buy organic vegetables, grass-fed beef, free-range chicken, and mercury-free fish. They can shop at more expensive grocery stores and dine at better restaurants. They eat higher quality food, but they also spend more *time* eating. And they can afford to eat in more tranquil environments, which is a big but often overlooked factor. The combination of making healthier choices and eating at a leisurely pace in pleasant surroundings results in better health and more enjoyment.

In this chapter, I am going to explore the world of eating rich. My premise, as with everything else I'm covering in this book, is that you can eat as well as a billionaire on a surprisingly limited budget.

Eating well, in this sense, means eating the best foods in the most enjoyable ways. It means developing eating habits that nourish your body and mind. It means looking forward to all of your meals—whether in or outside of your home.

What are the best foods? There are many ways to answer that question. But for the purposes of this book, let's say that the best foods are those that are not only delicious but also nutritious.

Delicious is, of course, a tricky qualifier. What is delicious to me might be disgusting to you. I am not going to attempt to persuade you to eat foods you don't enjoy. But I do want to point out that there is a difference between liking food because you like its taste and liking it because you have a craving for it.

For many people, chocolate cake is delicious. But if you think about the feeling you have when eating chocolate cake you may be able to distinguish between its flavor and the effect that starch and sugar has on your pleasure receptors.

Again, I'm not trying to persuade you to eliminate such empty calories from your diet. I'm simply pointing out that if you are conscious of the difference between food cravings and taste you may be able to make healthier choices.

Nutrition is a developing science. At one time, most of the information we received about the quality of food came from the government, and American industry funded and influenced its research. Back then, we were given a food pyramid that was extremely heavy in starches and other low-value carbohydrates. Nowadays, thanks to independent research, we know that the most nutritious foods are real foods—foods that Mother Nature intended for us to eat. These include free-range animals and organic fruits and vegetables. Such foods are somewhat more expensive. But as you will see as you read on, you can still include a generous portion of them in your diet without overspending.

It Doesn't Have to Be Expensive

Want to enjoy a billion-dollar meal?

Buy a half-bottle of Australian cabernet, a fresh baguette, a quarter-pound of ham, a wedge of good cheese, and a piece of fruit. Then go to a park, sit down beneath a tree, and have a peaceful hour-long lunch.

Or invite a few close friends over for an impromptu barbecue—steak and/or freshly caught fish grilled over hot coals. Serve it with a tossed organic salad and a bottle of California merlot or sauvignon blanc.

Or take a loved one to the best restaurant in town before the crowd gets there. Order several of your favorite appetizers and savor them, accompanied by a glass of wine. If you take your time, you'll be more than satisfied and will have spent less than half of what you would have spent on a full three-course dinner.

Eating rich is not about being fancy. And it's not about cost. It's about high-quality food and drink in a relaxing atmosphere with people you enjoy.

There is no food police watching you shop for groceries. No one cares if you buy frozen chicken nuggets instead of a farm-raised roaster. No one cares if you fill your cart with processed convenience foods instead of fresh fruits and vegetables.

The reason to buy quality food is that it tastes good and the quality of your life depends on it.

Cheap fuel gunks up cars. Junk food has the same effect on your body. It may provide some momentary comfort (as all bad habits do). But it forces your digestive system to work overtime to try to process it. That makes you tired and grumpy. And it makes you want to eat more junk.

Yesterday, I stopped at the market to pick up a few things. While I was checking over the organic avocados, a young couple walked up to the display. The girl picked up one of the avocados and said, "Oh, these look so good. Let's get some!"

The fellow, noticing the price, said, "Two for $5! No way!"

The girl put the avocado back, and they walked away.

I have no doubt that they spent at least $5 in the market that day. But it was probably on dead food that tastes like the box it came in. Food full of unhealthy fats and carbohydrates, rather than the healthy fats and vitamins in an avocado.

If you stay away from high-quality food because you think it's too expensive, this is a mindset that you need to lose. In the long run, it is actually cost-effective. For one thing, you eat less of it. More importantly, the hidden cost of eating poorly is reflected in the higher cost of health care. And when I say "health care," I include treatment for depression and anxiety.

So Where Do You Start?

Your first step is to get real. Literally.

Real Protein

Don't waste your hard-earned cash on hormone-laden, corn-fed beef from cattle raised in a feedlot. Grass-fed beef is lower in overall fat but has a much higher level of omega-3 fatty acids. In fact, the ratio of omega-3s to omega-6s is better than what you get from most fish.

The same goes for poultry. Free-range birds taste better and are a healthier choice. I encourage you to taste-test them yourself. You won't believe the difference. When it comes to seafood, look for wild-caught, coldwater fish. Responsible fish farming is coming on the scene, too.

Real Fruits and Vegetables

Nutritionally speaking, green and yellow vegetables are unbeatable—high in fiber and antioxidants. Go easy on potatoes and eat a minimum amount of corn. From a metabolic perspective, corn is pretty much the same as candy. It gives you a rush and it's addictive. Low-glycemic vegetables, on the other hand, keep insulin levels steady.

Organic produce is available in just about every grocery store. And in season, you'll find a wide variety of fruits and vegetables at your local farmers' markets, including tomatoes that really taste like tomatoes.

When you buy organic, it's not just about taste. Conventionally grown produce can be loaded with pesticides. And the risk of cross-contamination is so great that many grocers do not even store organics and conventional produce near each other.

Real Nuts and Seeds

Nuts—raw or toasted—are ideal snacks, full of protein, vitamins, and healthy fats. With only about 100 calories, ten almonds will tide you over—a cheaper, healthier choice than a candy bar. Nuts also add a nice crunch to a salad.

Note: You might want to steer clear of peanuts (which are actually legumes, not nuts). They are very high in calories. They are also susceptible to a mold that produces a carcinogen (aflatoxin) that has been linked to liver cancer.

Real Fat

As I mentioned, fat is a vital part of a healthy diet. You want real fat—from animals, eggs, avocados, and good oils. What you want to avoid is man-made trans fats, which are produced by hydrogenating liquid vegetable oils to make them solid. The result is a product with a very long shelf life. Good for your grocer, not so good for you.

Rule of thumb: Stay away from anything with the word "hydrogenated" on the label. That includes most margarines and processed foods.

The Red Meat Myth

For several decades, "red meat" has been associated with heart disease. The myth arose when early studies identified cholesterol as a cardiovascular villain.

In fact, there is nothing unhealthy about cholesterol.

Cholesterol is animal fat. And animal fat is a very good fat that fuels the body efficiently—as long as you stick with grass-fed, free-range meat. What you want to avoid is meat from animals that have been confined and pumped up with steroids and estrogen in order to fatten them up quickly.

And you don't have to pay a fortune for the good stuff, even when you eat out. Restaurants specializing in grass-fed, free-range meat are springing up everywhere.

Am I trying to talk you into eating beef even if you don't like it? No. My point is that there is a great deal of nutritional misinformation out there. As someone committed to healthy eating, I urge you to become familiar with the latest studies so you can make wise decisions about what to put into your body.

Hone Your Cooking Skills

I don't cook much and for a very good reason. K enjoys cooking and prepares delicious, healthy meals. What I've learned from watching her is that it doesn't take hours and dozens of ingredients to make a great meal. Nor does it require a lot of fancy equipment. One good, sharp knife is essential. A set of heavy-gauge pots and pans is an investment that will last a lifetime.

Roasting or grilling a piece of chicken or fish couldn't be easier. While it cooks, put together a salad or stir-fry some colorful veggies to go with it. A chunk of fresh, crusty bread rounds out the menu. For dessert? Maybe a perfectly ripe Asian pear.

When you know you'll be pressed for time, you can put something in your slow cooker before you leave the house for the day. By the time you return at suppertime, the aroma will be welcoming you home. Again, couldn't be easier.

And if you still have kids at home, get them involved in your efforts. Helping you with meal planning and preparation can be part of the quality time every family needs to spend together. At the very least, the entire family—no matter how busy everyone is—should sit down at the table three or four nights a week for good food and conversation. When our boys were still at home, this was a priority that we all honored and appreciated.

Eating well is much more than food for the body. It brings people together. It nourishes the soul. It works that way whether the meal is a picnic or a holiday spread. It works that way whether the wine costs $9 or $90.

Make it the best and most rewarding part of your day.

5 Tips for Restaurant Meals

I'm a big fan of "eating in." When done as a family, it can be a big part of a rich family life. I like eating at restaurants too. And when I do, I do my best to spend my money wisely.

Here's what I mean…

- When you want to try a very pricey restaurant, order just a glass of house wine and an appetizer. You'll get all of the ambience and service for a fraction of the money. An appetizer at a great restaurant is much more enjoyable than a big meal at some ordinary eatery. It's better for your soul—and your health.

- For business lunches, identify the very best place in town and become a regular customer. Learn the owner's name and get friendly with the staff. They'll always treat you like a VIP, even if all you ever order is the chopped salad.

- Try new places. It's easy to get stuck in a restaurant rut. If you notice a new place going in, even if it's a bit nondescript, stop in and check it out. Many ethnic places don't have the financial backing of a corporate franchise, and the food might be very authentic. You won't know if you don't give it a try.

- Watch for deals. Many of the restaurants we like have early bird specials—in some cases, half-price meals if you get there before 7:30. Others offer half portions, which are usually more than enough.

- Tip well. You might not spend a fortune in the restaurant, but you never want to appear cheap. Tip your server at least 15 to 20 percent *before* any coupons or discounts. Take care of the servers and they will take care of you.

4 Cuisines to Experiment With

If you were a billionaire, one of the perks you might indulge in would be to hire a personal chef. Think about it. You could "order" whatever kind of food you're in the mood for… host any number of unexpected guests at the drop of a hat… treat yourself, your family, and your friends to a superior dining experience every day of the week.

Nice, yes?

Living rich is all about having that kind of freedom. And it doesn't take a lot of money. What it does take is an interest in the food you eat to fuel your body and a willingness to experiment.

That said, here are four cuisines that are popular with those who can afford to eat anything they want: French, Italian, Chinese, and New American.

French: Small Portions of High-Quality Foods

The French have embraced moderation and *équilibre* (balance) in their diets. Portion sizes are small—on average, about 25 percent smaller than American portions. And though the French load their cuisine with butter, cream, and cheese, they eat more slowly than we do. As a result, they end up consuming fewer calories overall. Plus, they burn off a lot of calories with their lifestyle. The French designed their cities for walking, and they will almost always choose to take the stairs instead of an elevator.

An appreciation of the social aspects of dining is part of French culture. Street cafés and mom-and-pop brasseries encourage camaraderie and conversation. For the French, a meal is meant to be a shared experience, and it can last for hours.

Chinese: A Menu of Harmony and Balance

Chinese is one of the most popular cuisines in the world. However, most people are not familiar with its spiritual foundation. Two great philosophies, Confucianism and Taoism, contributed to the way the Chinese people prepare and serve food. From these philosophies came the concepts of harmony and balance—the importance of combining complementary meats and vegetables… hot and cold dishes… sweet and sour flavors.

New American Cuisine: Combining Farm-Fresh Ingredients With Culinary Creativity

New American cuisine has been described as fresh "down home" ingredients married to a cosmopolitan, upscale sensibility. Using seasonal ingredients from regional, organic, and sustainable farms, chefs toy with flavors and techniques. The result can be almost anything. In other words, New American cuisine is a very broad category.

You might see dishes like these on a typical menu:

- Cashew-Crusted Cod With Saffron Couscous and Vanilla Beurre Blanc

- Chili-Cinnamon Glazed Chilean Sea Bass

- Cuban Chicken With Black Bean and Chorizo Cassoulet

- Maple Braised Short Ribs With Horseradish Smashed Potatoes

Italian: A Diverse Culinary Experience

There are twenty distinct regions in Italy, and each has its own cuisine. Northern Italy, for example, has a colder climate. So its cuisine—risottos, gnocchi, and polenta—tends to be heavier. Much of Central Italy is on the seacoast, so it specializes in seafood. In the south, the cooking is more rustic. (This is where you find the pasta and pizza.)

The one thing they all have in common: The food is made from the freshest local ingredients.

So How Do I Eat—and How Should You Eat for Optimal Health and Energy?

I used to avoid red meat, eggs, butter, and ice cream. I used to eat whole grains with every meal—as the FDA's food pyramid told me I should. That seemed to work when I was young. But when I hit my forties, my weight ballooned up to 235 pounds.

Years later, I began a working relationship with Dr. Al Sears. When I started to follow his recommendations, I noticed an improvement in the way I felt right away.

Dr. Sears provides a complete plan of action in his book *The Doctor's Heart Cure*. Basically, he tells us to eat the way our cavemen ancestors ate. Here's the way he puts it in the book:

> *Remember those four basic food groups from grade school health class? If you've forgotten them, don't worry about it, they don't tell you anything about your natural diet. They were a nutritionist's attempt to make sense of a very contrived artificial diet based on grains and other processed foods....*
>
> *You don't have to count calories or record fat grams*

to achieve your ideal weight and maintain optimal cardiovascular health. All you have to do is to eat the same ratio and quality of proteins, fats, and carbohydrates that we have for eons. How are you going to do that? Get started by remembering these three easy principles:

Principle #1: Eat protein at every meal.

Principle #2: Limit carbohydrate intake.

Principle #3: Eat natural fats.

In simplest terms, this is what it means:

- Make quality protein the centerpiece of every meal. This should include non-contaminated fish such as wild salmon, sardines, or young tuna, as well as grass-fed meats, poultry, eggs, nuts, and beans.

- Eat a wide variety of herbs, leafy greens, and vegetables every day, as well as a moderate amount of fruit.

- Eat plenty of healthy fats. The best fats are in coldwater fish and fish oil. Nuts, eggs, and grass-fed beef also have good fats. Use olive oil and coconut oil.

- Avoid processed carbohydrates. In other words, don't eat anything made from grains or potatoes. Period. (If you can't imagine life without mashed potatoes, try pureed cauliflower.)

What you eat is a matter of personal choice. But to stay productive and energetic, try for a similar balance of fats, proteins, carbohydrates, and fiber.

Chapter 7

The Rich Man's Wine Cellar

There is a reason that champagne is associated with wealth: For most of the twentieth century in America, champagne was very expensive.

The same is true of the great red wines. How often in the books and movies that were popular in the 1970s and 1980s does the hero demonstrate his sophistication by ordering a vintage bordeaux?

When I was a child, Americans drank very little wine and produced even less. Then, sometime in my early teens (the 1960s), I began to see wine commercials on TV. Wine consumption increased steadily in the 1970s, but our consumption per capita couldn't compare with the French or the Italians. Even the English drank more than we did.

Wine's popularity soared in the 1980s and 1990s as baby boomers came into their maturity. Today, the U.S. is the largest consumer and fourth-largest producer in the world.

Australia, New Zealand, and South Africa, too—aided by sunny climates—became major producers, consumers, and exporters. Then Argentina and Chile got into the game. I can't think of a country I've visited in the past ten years (including India and Thailand) that doesn't produce at least some local wine.

As the wine industry grew, so did a subset of the wine-drinking population who appreciated good wine. In my college years, there were few books in English about wine and no magazines that I knew of. Today, there are hundreds of books and more than a dozen magazines.

Twenty years ago, the "big" American producers (e.g., Gallo) catered to a relatively unsophisticated palate. Table wines were the rule and white and rosé wines were more popular than reds.

Today, any decent-sized wine store has dozens of good choices in every category—from American cabernets to Italian Barolos to Australian merlots.

The market is large and the competition is fierce. And that means you don't have to spend a lot of money to have a full and rich enjoyment of wine.

The secret to drinking wine like a billionaire is to have a good familiarity with the types of wines available and to know which of them you like. But keep in mind that enjoying wine—and this is true of most areas of enjoyment—is a process of continual change. The wine you most enjoy at the outset of your education is unlikely to be the wine you enjoy years later.

The goal is not to become a wine connoisseur but to get to the point where you feel confident buying wine for home consumption and ordering wine when you dine out.

Price vs. Quality

Our mission here is the same as always: to examine how rich-minded people enjoy wine and to identify world-class wine that you can buy on a modest (i.e., intelligent) budget.

The first thing to know about wine is this: The price of a bottle of wine does not determine its quality.

Blind taste tests have proven this over and over again. In 1976, for example, Steven Spurrier, a British wine merchant, organized a tasting of wines from France and California. Much to the surprise of the eleven experts on the tasting panel, four relatively inexpensive cabernets from Napa Valley beat out much costlier contenders from such illustrious vineyards as Mouton Rothschild and Haut-Brion.

When the same tasting was repeated a few years later, an inexpensive cabernet from Napa Valley topped the list once again. (It's these two well-publicized events, by the way, that put Napa

Valley on the wine world map.)

More recently, Mouton Rothschild and Haut-Brion were pitted against American upstarts. This time, the American wines were from New Jersey. And though the Jersey wines didn't quite come out on top, they ran a close second. The cost of those Jersey wines? On average, about 5 percent of their French counterparts.

If you could be a fly on the wall of a fancy restaurant in Manhattan, you'd notice three very distinct types of wine drinkers.

1. The baffled and/or intimidated. They don't know a thing about wine and they don't pretend to. The brave ones will call on the sommelier, tell him how much they wish to pay, and then ask for recommendations. This is the smart option. The timid ones will look at the list and pick a bottle based on the name ("This one sounds kind of classy.") and the price (I'll pay ten bucks more than I want to so the waiter won't roll his eyes.").

2. The pretenders. These are people who select wines that are generally considered to be very good by other pretenders. If they are looking for a red wine and Opus One is on the menu, they will order that. If champagne is called for, they will order Dom Pérignon or Cristal. They are slaves to brand advertising because they don't really know what they like and are afraid to admit it. They are happy to pay more than they should to impress their friends or colleagues.

3. The honest enthusiasts. They like drinking wine and they also enjoy learning about wine, but they don't pretend to be connoisseurs. They read about wine now and then. They ask questions when they are at restaurants. They are open to experimenting. But they never spend more than their budget allows.

My purpose here is to help you avoid the silly mistakes the pretenders make and enjoy a life of wine drinking without stressing your budget. And though I wouldn't normally quote Donald Trump on anything to do with living rich, he is right when he says this in his book *Trump: Think Like a Billionaire: Everything You Need to Know About Success*: "It's nice that people think Dom Pérignon is a good champagne, because it is. But it isn't the best…. Always remember that the most famous doesn't always equal the best. The best is a quest."

6 Common Myths About Wine

Myth #1: Good wine is expensive.

Countless blind taste tests have proven the fallacy of this idea. (A blind taste test is one in which the experts do not know the variety or brand or vintage of the wines they are tasting.) Every blind test I've read about includes, among the favorites, several bottles of inexpensive wine (less than $20 per bottle).

Myth #2: Red wine is better than white wine, and white wine is better than rosé.

I don't know where this idea came from, but it is silly. When I hear someone say, "I drink only red wine," I think, "This guy knows nothing about wine." I have the same thought when someone talks about rosé as if it were somehow illegitimate. The fact is that there are plenty of great white and rosé wines. And sometimes they are better suited to a meal than reds.

Myth #3: Ignore the rules about matching wine with food. Drink what you like.

This is a myth that cropped up among American wine advocates. It sounds smart and egalitarian. But I can assure you that after you have tasted many bottles of wine you will come to the conclusion that the old rules about pairing wine with food make a lot of sense.

Myth #4: It doesn't matter what sort of glass you drink from.

Here I might be accused of pseudo-sophistication. There have been a few studies that demonstrated that most wine drinkers cannot detect any difference between a wine that is sipped from a proper wine glass and one that is sipped from a mayonnaise jar. It is also true that the French and Italians—people who have always enjoyed wine as an essential part of their lives—sometimes use simple glassware. But when you are drinking a good wine, one you intend to savor, I recommend a stemmed glass. And not just any stemmed glass but one that is appropriate to the kind of wine you are drinking. You want a stemmed glass because you don't want your fingers to heat the wine while you drink it. You want the right sort of glass because you care about how much of the bouquet is available when you smell it. And you want thin glass because it simply feels better against your lips. I can't prove it, but I believe it's true.

Myth #5: Cork corks are superior.

The traditional wine cork is made from cork. And some traditionalists argue that cork corks are better. In fact, synthetic corks are better at preserving wine than cork corks. And bottle caps—the most undignified of all—are better still.

Myth #6: Good wine is aged wine.

The fact is, only a small percentage of wine varieties get better with age. French bordeaux and non-French cabernet sauvignons certainly do. So do French burgundies and non-French pinot noirs. Most rosés and white wines don't need aging. The same is true of many red wines. Any basic wine book will explain all of this very adequately.

Educating Your Palate

There are three major factors that determine the flavor of wine. One is geography. Different areas have different climates and different soils. Another is the grape variety. A cabernet sauvignon grape is different than a merlot grape, and a merlot grape is different than a pinot noir grape. The third is the manufacturing process. When and how the grapes are harvested and how they are fermented and aged are important.

As you try different wines, you will find that you favor certain regions, grapes, and manufacturing processes over others. But don't be surprised if those initial preferences change as you try many more.

Broadly speaking, there are two categories of wines:

- Red (made from red grapes)

- White (usually made from white grapes but can be made from red grapes too)

The Reds

There are hundreds of varieties of red grapes, but only a handful are used in producing most red wines. Here they are, from the lightest and least tannic to the boldest and heavier-bodied:

Gamay (France)—Used to produce beaujolais. Dominant flavors: strawberry, raspberry, and cherry.

Pinot Noir (France)—Used to produce burgundy and champagne. This is a notoriously hard grape to grow. Its thin skins damage easily, and the plant reacts wildly to changing weather. Dominant flavors: black cherry, raspberry, currant, spice.

Tempranillo (Spain)—The traditional wine produced with this grape is garnet colored and tastes of tea, vanilla, and brown sugar. The modern version has a darker color and tastes of plums and tobacco.

Sangiovese (Tuscany, Italy)—Used to produce chianti and brunello di montalcino. Dominant flavors: cherry, anise, and tobacco.

Merlot (France)—Usually blended with other grapes. Dominant flavors: watermelon, cherry, and plum.

Zinfandel (California)—Produces a dry red wine as well as a medium-sweet rosé (also known as "white zinfandel"). Dominant flavors: raspberry, black cherry, raisin.

Cabernet Sauvignon (France)—The primary grape in French bordeaux and an important grape in Napa Valley. Dominant flavors: currant and black cherry.

Syrah/Shiraz (France/Australia)—It's syrah in France, shiraz in Australia. Same grape, though the Australian wines produced with it are more full-bodied. Dominant flavors: blackberry, plum, pepper, and clove.

The Whites

Nine out of ten white wines are produced by three varieties of grapes. From the lightest to the fullest-bodied, they are:

Riesling (Germany)—Wine produced from this grape can be dry, medium-dry, or downright sweet. (Those with a very high sugar level are delicious… and very expensive.) Dominant flavors: floral and citrus.

Sauvignon Blanc (France)—This grape is a chameleon. It has a combination of fruity (lime, peach) and herbaceous (pepper, grass) flavors. And depending on how ripe the grape is, one of those flavors will be dominant.

Chardonnay (France)—Though France (Burgundy) is chardonnay's motherland, this very adaptable grape is grown worldwide and produces many popular (and inexpensive) white wines. Dominant flavors: oak, apple, pear, citrus, and melon.

Reading the Label

Here's what to look for:

- **Producer**—who made the wine. When you find a wine that you like, you'll want to look for more from that same producer.

- **Vintage**—the year the grapes were harvested. If the grapes are from more than one year, the designation is NV (non-vintage). Keep in mind that older is not necessarily better. Some wines are meant to be drunk young, while others need to be "cellared" for years. Still, some vintages are better than others, and the price of the wine will reflect that.

- **Location**—which can include region and vineyard. The more specific the information, the better the wine (generally speaking). Example: Napa Valley is better than California.

- **Grape Variety or Appellation**—Wines from the "Old World" (France, Italy, and Spain) are identified by *appellation*. The label tells you where the grapes were grown—e.g., burgundy, chianti, rioja. Wines from the "New World" (the United States, Australia, South Africa, New Zealand, and Chile) are *varietal*. The label tells you the name(s) of the grapes used to make them—e.g., chardonnay, merlot, zinfandel.

- **"Estate Bottled"**—When you see "Estate Bottled" on the label, this tells you that the growers of 100 percent of the grapes produced and bottled the wine. A very good sign. Almost as good: "Produced and Bottled By," which tells you that the bottler fermented at least 75 percent of the wine.

Starting Your Wine Collection

I love walking into my cellar and picking out the perfect bottle of wine to accompany a meal. If you don't feel the same way, forget wine and take up a collection of something else that gives you great pleasure.

Assuming you are open to exploring many different wines, I recommend aiming for a beginning collection of about 50 bottles. It might have the following components:

- Red Wines: 20 bottles

- White Wines: 20 bottles

- Rosé Wines: 4-5 bottles

- Fortified Wines: 3 bottles—In particular, I would recommend a bottle-aged port (which matures wonderfully), and two sherries (dry and sweet).

- Sparkling Wines: 2-3 bottles (to keep on hand for special occasions)

> *Note:* Technically, to be labeled "champagne," a wine must meet the strict rules and regulations set by the Comité Interprofessionnel du Vin de Champagne (CIVC). And you can spend a huge amount of money on the real stuff. But if all you want is fizz in your glass to toast the New Year or a newly engaged couple, there are some very good—very reasonably priced—sparkling wines produced in Spain (cava), Italy (prosecco and asti), and California.

Breaking this down further, you could divide the whites and reds into three categories each: light, medium, and full-bodied.

- Light Reds: 4 bottles

- Medium Reds: 6 bottles

- Heavy Reds: 10 bottles

- Light Whites: 6 bottles

- Aromatic Whites: 8 bottles

- Heavy Whites: 6 bottles

Now, where are you going to put all that wine?

Storage Options

The important thing is to keep the wine away from light and as close to 60 degrees as possible. Heat will turn the wine bad. Humidity is another factor to consider. A higher humidity level (ideally 65 to 75 percent) helps to keep oxygen from seeping in through a shrinking cork. Storing the wine on its side will also help prevent the cork from shrinking and drying up.

Most California wines and wines that cost less than $25 per bottle are meant to be drunk within two years. A simple storage rack or countertop wine cooler will let you keep these wines on hand while you find out if you are interested in a more serious investment.

But as your investment in your collection grows, you'll want to start looking at other options. To pick the right one for your needs, here are some things to consider:

- **How many bottles will you want to store?** Keep in mind that your collection will continue to grow. Also keep in mind that wider bottles or bottles with long necks will cut down the capacity of the unit.

- **What kind of wine will you be storing?** Dual-zone units give you the flexibility to store red and white wines at different temperatures.

- **Door construction.** A glass door makes it easier to see the wine, but a solid door is usually better insulated (and more expensive). Sunlight can damage wine, so if the unit has a glass door, it should have a UV-protective tinted finish.

- **Interior construction.** An aluminum interior is best for maintaining temperature, but wood is fine too, so long as it is tightly paneled and unvarnished.

- **Shelving.** Shelves that roll out and tilt are convenient for reading labels and removing bottles. Some units have adjustable shelves to accommodate unusual bottle sizes and shapes.

- **Security.** A unit with an integrated lock will help protect your investment. Some models will sound an alarm when the door is left open.

- **Vibration.** Compressors, even those labeled "silent," tend to vibrate slightly and make noise—and vibration can wreck a wine. So you'll want a unit with coated racks that grip the bottles and a compressor that's mounted on rubber blocks.

- **Ventilation.** Some units need 5 inches or more of space for ventilation. Make sure you have enough room for this.

For the ultimate long-term storage, a wine "cellar" is ideal. Your cellar can be as small as half of a coat closet or as large as a warehouse, depending on your needs and your budget.

You might, for example, convert part of your garage or basement into a reach-in wine cellar. How much would that cost? Well, a custom-built 8-by-8-foot space—with a self-contained cooling unit, room for racking on three walls, tile flooring, and an insulated door—might run about $15,000.

Keep in mind that you don't need to cellar wines with short life spans. You'll want to stock some choices for everyday pairings with meals. But if you invest in a cellar, you should start collecting wines that will age. (Don't go overboard. Remember, your taste will change, and you don't want to be stuck with a lot of wine you no longer enjoy.)

Reds are more suitable for aging due to their high tannin content. Over time, the tannins mellow out and become a complex background for the fruit flavors. Wines that have a track record for aging include bordeaux, burgundies, rhônes, and vintage ports. Other good candidates for aging are the Italian chiantis and Spanish riojas.

However, when you're just starting out, don't obsess about storage. Put a case in a closet or the basement and start building a collection of wines you really like to drink. As you learn more about wine and your collection grows, you can invest in some proper storage. By that time, you will have a better idea of just how many bottles you want to store. Novices typically underestimate how quickly the cellar will be filled. So doubling or even tripling the number of bottles you expect to accumulate is not unreasonable.

Establish *Your* Personal Preferences

I'm not a fan of systems for "scoring" wine, and there are many. One of the most popular is Robert Parker's 100-point system, which was adopted by *Wine Spectator* magazine. The problem with that system is this: Originally, a score of 60 or above was considered acceptable. Then, over time, a score of 80 became the commercial benchmark. Wines scoring lower than that are now considered unacceptable. As a result, consumers ignore a lot of good wines that are excellent buys.

I'm not a fan of wine competitions either, but that is how a lot of wine gets marketed. Consumers who don't know what they like feel good about buying something that's won an award.

Yes, wine scores can be helpful, but take them with a grain of salt. You don't need someone to score your produce or your shoes before you buy them, so don't make wine scores more important than they are.

Taste is a matter of personal preference. You have to do your homework and find out what types and styles of wine please your palate.

When you find one you like, buy a few bottles for your cellar. If you really love it, buy a case.

The Wine Tasting "Ritual"

You don't need to put on a big act to enjoy wine. You don't need to sniff the cork. And you don't need to decant young wine (less than, say, seven or eight years old). But there is something to be said for the traditional wine-tasting protocol. Learning to taste wine properly will increase the enjoyment you get from it. It will also educate you on what you like and don't like so you can buy or order wine with confidence.

Here's how to do it:

1. Tasting actually begins with your eyes. You can learn a good deal about a wine simply by observing its color. So to begin the ritual, pour a small amount of wine into your glass.

Now hold the glass up to the light to see the color of the wine. White wines deepen to gold or yellow-brown as they age. Reds change from purplish or ruby red to brick red or brown. Deeply colored wines are usually bolder in taste, while lighter ones are less so.

As a beginner, you simply want to notice whether the wine you're about to drink is light or dark… whether the color is uniform or lighter/darker at the edges. You'll find that some wines taste better when they are new, and some taste better when they are old (assuming they've been cellared properly). A rich, glossy color with subtle gradations toward the rim is usually a better wine.

2. Put your nose to the glass and sniff the wine. At first, this may feel sort of ostentatious. But, in fact, much of the pleasure of wine comes from its "bouquet" (aroma).

3. After that initial sniff, swirl the wine in the glass to "oxidate" it… and take another sniff. See if the bouquet has changed at all. Is it more mellow? Maybe. Maybe not. The point is to be conscious of the change if a change has occurred.

4. Now you get to taste. Take a sip, but don't gulp it down. Hold the wine in your mouth for a moment to warm it up and release even more aroma into the nasal passages. Then swallow it, noting how it tastes immediately and in the seconds that follow.

Was it overly sweet or acidic or tannic? Or was it a nice balance of each of those things? How long did the taste linger? One sign of a quality wine is a long, pleasing aftertaste for up to several minutes.

Ordering Wine in a Restaurant

My first rule when ordering wine in a restaurant is this: In a restaurant that has a good but expensive wine list, I order the least expensive bottle of the variety I want. I do that because I know that any sommelier worth his salt will not allow a bad wine to appear on his list. In such a restaurant, the cheapest wine is often the best value. If the wine list is not so good, I order a known brand at the price point I know it should be.

Here are my other rules:

- Be careful when ordering chardonnay. This is currently America's favorite wine, and restaurants charge accordingly. You're likely to get a much better price on a riesling or a sauvignon blanc.

- Never order Santa Margherita pinot grigio. It's the most popular imported wine in the country, and restaurants mark up the price due to its popularity. It is not uncommon to pay triple the wholesale cost for this wine. Look for a better value on the wine list. And if you still want the Santa Margherita, buy a bottle at your local retailer to drink at home.

- Check the vintage of the bottle you receive. If the restaurant inventory isn't turning over very quickly, you could end up with a vintage that hasn't been stored well… or is just past its prime, period. If you notice a switch, just tell the waiter you'd prefer the year you asked for.

- Don't ignore house wines offered by the bottle or carafe. This is common practice in Europe, and some American restaurants are getting on board. Try it if it's an option.

- If you're hosting a business dinner, take a few precautionary steps to look more informed and in control at the restaurant. Check out the wine list in advance, either online or ask the restaurant to send you a copy to review. You can research options at your convenience. Or arrive at the restaurant fifteen or twenty minutes ahead of your guests and talk to the sommelier privately.

- One more piece of advice: Sommeliers can be great allies. Treat them with professional courtesy. Asking for advice when faced with a varied and lengthy wine list is not a sign of weakness. However, give your sommelier some specific guidelines on approximately how much money you want to spend and any preferences that will help you end up with a wine you truly like.

- On rare occasions, the wine will taste like vinegar. That means the wine has gone bad. It is undrinkable, and you should return it. But you should never return a wine simply because you don't love the taste. That is the ultimate sign of an amateur. The only exception is when the sommelier (or waiter) has recommended the wine to you and you ask him, before he opens the bottle, if you can return it if you don't like it.

A Few Words About Liquor and Beer...

Wine is certainly at the top of my list, but I've learned to appreciate certain other beverages.

Single-malt scotch is one of them. And nowadays, you can add vodka and bourbon and tequila to that list. And, finally, there is beer—good, old beer.

Liquor

As with wine, there are many kinds and brands of liquor to choose from.

Rich but unsophisticated liquor drinkers tend to buy the most expensive bottles on the shelves because they assume there is a direct correlation between quality and price. By now, you know that is not always true. To enjoy liquor, you must do pretty much what I recommended for wine. Spend some time learning about it. Then find out what you like by doing a lot of tasting—"neat" or on the rocks, please. Maybe with a splash of club soda or water.

Taste scotch and whiskey and bourbon and the white liquors. See how you like the taste, and then see how you feel later. I've never understood why (although I'm sure there is an explanation), but liquor tends to affect people in different ways. I have found that dark liquors make me feel cloudy. Rum makes me angry. The light liquors are sometimes good and sometimes bad for me. The best one for me is tequila. And there are dozens of very good tequilas to choose from.

So begin by finding what kind of liquor gives you the best overall experience. That experience includes the taste, the initial feeling, and how you feel afterward. Don't assume that the liquor you prefer now is the one that is best suited to you. It may be. But you won't know until you've tested others.

And if it turns out that a fifteen-year-old single-malt scotch really is your favorite, go ahead and treat yourself. When you consider that you'll get sixteen shots out of a bottle, that makes it a luxury you can afford.

Beer

For most of my life, beer occupied a lower station in my imagination. But recently I became a partner in a microbrewery in my hometown. As a result, I have been tasting beer regularly and have been impressed with how many different sorts of beers there are.

Because I like my beer cold, I tend to prefer beers with distinctive flavors. (Chilling tends to mute the taste of any beverage.) And because I seldom drink more than two beers at a sitting, I prefer beers that have higher alcoholic content.

For these reasons, I'm not a fan of the most popular American beers, such as Budweiser, Coors, and Miller. I feel unpatriotic for not liking them, but I don't. Nor do I like all of the pseudo-exotic American beers, such as Samuel Adams and Sierra Nevada. Most of them are the same quality beer in different bottles. And when the taste does differ a bit, it is generally for the worse.

The beers I like are usually imported beers—not the lighter ones, such as Pilsner Urquell, Heineken, and Stella Artois—but the darker and stronger ones, such as Negra Modelo, Dos Equis (dark), and Tsingtao. I've also checked out (and enjoyed) many regional microbrews.

As for as drinking beer like a billionaire, I have a few ideas. None of these are more than prejudices. Accept them for that.

- Beer is not a drink that goes with everything. To drink beer "richly," you have to pair it properly—so it enhances rather than diminishes or competes with the food. It doesn't go well with fine Italian, Spanish, or French cuisine. But it does work with the heavier cuisines you find in Germany and Eastern Europe. It also goes well with spicy Asian dishes. And, of course, it is a must with hot dogs and Mexican food.

- The first cold beer is the best beer. The second beer will give you half the pleasure, and the third will give you half of that. This is exactly the opposite of good wine, which seems to get better with each consecutive glass.

- Drink one beer and sometimes two, but never more than two.

- Never drink beer and wine at the same meal. (I have a friend who actually drinks beer, wine, and Coke at dinner. Horrors!)

And, finally...

- Never, ever get drunk on beer. It is sloppy and low-class.

Chapter 8

The Rich Man's Wardrobe

The idea of dressing like a billionaire is questionable. How do billionaires dress?

When I think of billionaires I think of Warren Buffett, Steve Jobs, and Donald Trump. Buffett dresses like a bewildered college professor. Steve Jobs dressed as if he could never decide whether he was a boy or man, a visionary or a geek. And Donald Trump? He dresses well if you go for that dark-suit, red-tie, I'm-going-to-be-president-one-day look.

So why should you want to dress like a billionaire? The answer is that you shouldn't. Your goal should be to dress well—really well—as well as you could if money were no object. And (as you will not be surprised to know) you can do that without spending a lot of money.

Why Bother?

If you have a billion dollars, you can dress like Warren Buffett and people will still respect and admire you. But if you have ordinary wealth (that is to say, not a lot of wealth), dressing well has its advantages.

First and foremost, dressing well makes you look better. If you are chubby, it makes you look slimmer. If you are short, it makes you look taller. If you are tall and thin—hell, if you are tall and thin (and young), you look good in anything. You can skip the rest of this chapter. Except that dressing well also makes you feel good.

And that's a good reason to dress well, don't you think? So that you can feel comfortable and even happy with your appearance when you venture out into the world?

Understand that the advice you will be getting in this chapter isn't coming from me directly. (I have no training in or natural talent for dressing well.) It's based on what I've learned by following the advice of people who make a living by dressing wealthy and successful people.

Still, the general thesis I'm proposing is the same. You can dress rich by dressing classically, suitably, and avoiding extremes. That doesn't necessarily mean conservatively, as I'll explain. It just means that you don't want to dress like Austin Powers or Phyllis Diller.

The Fundamental Rules

Many people equate dressing rich with designer clothing. But there is nothing more foolish, in my humble opinion, than to spend tons of money on designer clothing when you are living on a budget.

Another bad idea is "fast fashion"—cheap but trendy outfits that can be bought at stores that have cropped up to serve the cheap-but-trend-following consumer. Fast fashion is like fast food. It's inexpensive and it gives you a quick fix, but it is not necessarily good for you.

And yet another bad idea is typically American: favoring quantity over quality. According to the American Apparel and Footwear Association, the average person buys 68 garments and 8 pairs of shoes every year.

There is a better way.

You can dress well and feel very good in your clothes without spending a lot of money. All you have to do is follow two simple rules that will improve your wardrobe and save you a fortune spent on the wrong things.

1. Buy quality clothing, but don't buy it at full price. Buy when it is discounted by at least 50 percent or buy it secondhand.

2. Never buy anything—no matter whose name is on the label or how cheap it is—if it doesn't make you look *and* feel good when you put it on.

Where to Make It Happen

Consignment Shops—especially those that specialize in designer labels. You can get great buys on high-end, "gently used" garments.

Thrift Stores—not as easy to score here as with consignment shops but well worth the time it takes to check out the merchandise.

Outlet Malls—but keep in mind that most designers have a secondary line that they produce just for the outlets. They usually change the label slightly, so make sure you know what you're getting.

Discount Chains—stores like Marshalls and TJ Maxx have made serious business out of selling designer overstock at significantly reduced prices.

The only time you should shop at luxury department stores and boutiques is when they are having a big sale and are selling their clothes cheaply. And I mean really cheaply. Fifty percent full price, as I said, is the maximum you should consider paying for designer clothes. And if you are smart about it, you can pay only half that much. Sometimes even less.

Whether you're buying secondhand or brand-new (but on sale), the trick, of course, is to know what you're looking for:

- Clothing that will last—garments that are very well made and classically styled

- Clothing that fits you perfectly (or can be easily tailored)

- Clothing that makes you feel as good as you look when you put it on

---

Put Your Wardrobe on a Diet

To dress well, a man does not need more than six or seven types of shoes. A woman will need a few more—but certainly no more than a dozen. (Don't quote me on this. I'm generalizing. But you get the point.) But according to a poll conducted by *Time* magazine, men own an average of 12 pairs of shoes. Women own an average of 27 pairs of shoes and more than 10 handbags.

In this regard, I must confess, my feminine side prevails. I must have 40 pairs of shoes. To me, each one is different. But even my wife can't tell the difference between one pair of black penny loafers and another. ("Can't you see how much wider that band is?")

This addiction to shoes doesn't help me dress better. It is a hindrance. For one thing, I can't see all of my choices just by looking into my closet. The shoes that end up toward the back get ignored for months or even years at a time. For another thing, the selection process is stressful. Had I fewer choices, I know I could make quicker and more confident decisions.

I'm doing better with the other things in my closet. I used to have more than 60 dress shirts. A third of them didn't even fit me. Another third were in colors that made me look half dead. After seeing those forty losers taking up space for several years, I finally got rid of them. It was weirdly difficult. I had some strange emotional attachment to them. But the moment they were gone I felt better. I could open my closet door and know that every shirt in front of me would look and fit well.

A few weeks after my shirt purge, I did the same thing with my pants, taking a collection of about forty pairs down to twenty. Again, the culling was a little difficult, but the result was positive.

Sometime soon I'm going to do the same thing with my T-shirts, golf clothes, and belts. (My shoes… I don't know.)

As James Dion, author of *The Complete Idiot's Guide to Starting and Running a Retail Store*, suggests, we should all pay attention to the De Beers' slogan: "Fewer Better Things."

Choose Quality Over Quantity

If you have never worn a quality garment, you may doubt that there is much of a difference. From a distance, a cocktail dress from H&M might look as good as one from Saks Fifth Avenue. But up close, the difference is obvious.

Seams and Hems—Stitches should be tight and close together, not loose or broken. Hems should be generous. If there's a pattern on the fabric, it should line up neatly at the seams.

Linings—Skirts, suits, jackets, and trousers that are lined tend to be higher-quality garments. They glide onto the body easily and hang better than those that are unlined.

Reinforcements—Buttons, zippers, and pockets should be reinforced for wear. Pockets should be sewn to the lining. Zippers should be lined and invisibly set into the garment.

Fabrics—Wool, silk, cotton, and linen are always best. Sometimes newer garments will have a bit of synthetic mixed in for durability.

Trim—Synthetic lace is a dead giveaway that the piece is not well made. If the trim is skimpy, so is the cut and fabric. Plastic belts and base-metal buckles look like what they are.

By stocking your closet with quality clothes, you enjoy several benefits. You will have the comfort of knowing that they are all well-made. That, I've noticed, actually feels good. You will also have the economic benefit of endurance. Quality clothes last longer than inexpensive knockoffs. Sometimes five times as long.

The Cost of Possession

In Chapter 2, I explained the difference between price and cost of use. Price is the initial expense of purchasing something. But cost of use is how much you actually pay over the lifetime of possessing it. The two are almost always radically different.

Here's the problem. When you shop all the time and buy cheap clothes, you spend a lot of money on a bunch of stuff that you're not going to want to own long-term. So when you do run across a good buy on a quality item, you've already blown your budget. Basically, you've thrown your money away.

Changing your mindset is the first step. Instead of tossing $20 here and $20 there, save it up. When you put on a garment made of great fabric and it fits well—it just feels different. It will be a piece you will want to keep and wear again and again because you will feel good in it. And it will be cheaper in the long run.

Choose Natural Over Synthetic

Clothing manufacturers have done wonders with synthetic fabrics. They are easy and inexpensive to work with and can sometimes resemble natural materials.

But natural fabrics have natural advantages. They have characteristics that make them distinctive and memorable. And they last longer without looking shabby.

Polyester is made of oil, just like plastic grocery bags. Elizabeth Cline, author of *Overdressed: The Shockingly High Cost of Cheap Fashion*, says: "It's ironic that people take their plastic bags back to the grocery store to be recycled but they fill their closets with clothing made from the same thing."

So start thinking of your wardrobe as an investment—not as a disposable part of your life.

Classics—the Foundation of Your Wardrobe

People known for their taste in clothing have learned what works for them. They have figured out what to include in their wardrobes. And, just as importantly, what to leave out. They are suspicious of fashion trends. They understand that when you follow a trend, you tell the world that you are a sheep and not an individual. They favor classical pieces, but they are not afraid to experiment with bits and pieces that make their particular style of dressing unique.

My feeling is that 80 percent of your wardrobe should be classics… items that you can keep for ten years without worrying about them going out of style. The other 20 percent should be items that define your personal "look."

What makes the classics so valuable as the foundation of your wardrobe is their simplicity and elegance. They are timeless for a reason: You can wear them again and again, making them look different simply by changing your accessories. And the image that you present to the world will always be positive.

Do you remember when former San Francisco 49ers' coach Mike Nolan fought to be able to wear a business suit during football games? Why did he do it? Because he wanted everyone to be able to see him as the man in charge.

That's what clothes—the right clothes—can do for you.

Wardrobe Essentials for Men

No matter what your lifestyle is, there are several things that every man should own:

- 1 suit

- 1 blazer or sport jacket

- 3 ties

- 2 pairs of jeans

- 1 pair of dark slacks

- 1 pair of chinos

- 4 dress shirts

- 4 sport shirts

- 1 pair of casual shoes

- 1 pair of dress shoes

- 12 pairs of socks

- 1 trench coat

If you own only one suit, make it a dark color. Black, gray, or navy in 100 percent wool is the most versatile. The classic style that always looks modern is a two-button jacket with a narrow lapel.

Your basic dress shirts should be solid white or blue in a cotton fabric that is easy to launder.

For your dress shoes, choose a pair of black lace-ups. For your casual shoes, choose a pair of loafers in brown or black.

Good socks are a must. They should cushion your foot, not ride down or bunch up. (I'm partial to cashmere…)

Dark trousers are fairly formal and can be paired with a classic navy blazer or sport jacket. Chinos are more casual but dressier than jeans. As for jeans, go for a dark wash that will look good with either a dress shirt or a cotton T-shirt. A classic navy blazer will look sharp with the dress slacks, the chinos, or the jeans.

Michael Haney of *GQ* magazine says the only jeans he wears are Levi's 501. They are thirty bucks a pair and last for years. But he points out that sometimes "expensive" is actually the better deal: "I've gotten more than a few shirts custom-made at Charvet in Paris," he says. "Sure, the initial outlay is big. But consider this: These are shirts that are cut by hand from exclusive fabrics and then hand sewn with an insanely high degree of craftsmanship.

These are shirts that will last forever and are unique to me. I'm not a financier, but all I can say is, 'Dude, amortize that!'"

Wardrobe Essentials for Women

Women tend to have way too many clothes. And in spite of that, they often stand in front of the closet in despair, thinking they have nothing to wear. The answer to this problem is to start with a core wardrobe of neutral-colored classics and build from there. Your core wardrobe might include:

- 1 pencil skirt
- 1 "little black dress"
- 2 pairs of jeans
- 2 pairs of dress pants, dark and light
- 4 blouses
- 4 casual tops
- 3 sweaters
- 1 jacket
- 2 pairs of casual shoes
- 1 pair of dress shoes
- 1 trench coat

The idea is to dress to emphasize your assets and cover up your figure flaws. So, for example, if you have a short neck, you'll want to choose v-neck tops to elongate your neckline. If you have great legs, you'll want to wear short skirts to show them off.

A pencil skirt is flattering on almost all body types. So are single-breasted coats and jackets.

When shopping for jeans and casual pants, here are a few guidelines:

- straight leg—looks good on everyone

- wide leg—good on women with big bottoms and fuller figures

- boot-cut —good on women with long legs, pear shapes

- narrow leg—good on women with slim legs, petite frames

For your dress shoes, choose a pair of black pumps. For your casual shoes, choose ballet flats and/or loafers.

For your jacket, choose one that can be paired with the skirt, the dress pants, and the jeans.

And be careful with the bling. Too much looks gaudy, no matter how expensive it is. Classic equals understated.

Finally, a few words on the subject of black. Black is figure-flattering. Black is elegant. Black is timeless… and always a good choice.

Make It Fit

Even an expensive garment can look cheap if it doesn't fit well. And a moderately priced garment can look expensive when it is tailored to your body.

A skilled tailor is the secret behind many people who consistently appear on "best dressed" lists. He understands different body types and knows how to make yours look a little taller and slimmer by taking a tuck here and a tuck there. He knows exactly how long a skirt, a pair of trousers, and a sleeve should be. And a good tailor will tell you when something is not worth the money it would take for alterations.

Take Care of Your Investment

In 1997, Sotheby's sold some of the belongings of the Duke and Duchess of Windsor. The collection included clothing that had been made for the Duke in the 1920s... that he still wore well into the 1970s. This speaks not only to the quality of the garments but also to how well they were taken care of.

Here are a few tips to keep your clothing looking as good as it did the day you bought it:

- *Brush suit coats, dresses, skirts, and trousers after each wearing.* This takes about 30 seconds and will really make a difference in how long the garment lasts. A clean brush with stiff bristles will remove dust and dirt before it can settle into the fabric. Give it a good brushing and let it air out overnight before putting it back in the closet.

- *Make repairs as needed.* If you notice a loose button, fix it before you lose it. If you notice a small tear in a seam, mend it before it gets any bigger.

- *Ditch the wire hangers.* About the only use for a wire hanger that I can think of is to open a car door if you lock your keys inside. It certainly isn't something you want to hang a $300 jacket on. Invest in wooden hangers that are least one inch thick at the shoulders. It's a small price to pay.

- *Have wool garments professionally cleaned.* Moths love wool. And they can eat it to shreds. Never pack wool clothing away without having it treated for storage. If the chemicals are objectionable to you, find a cleaner that uses a natural process.

Spend Time, Not Money

Like I said, the foundation of your wardrobe should be classics—timeless garments that you can wear for years.

It's not difficult to buy a beautiful, high quality (Armani, say) suit (or dress) at a consignment shop for $400 and have it tailored to fit you perfectly for another $100. You'd have something that would give you pleasure every time you wore it and you could wear it for thirty years.

Or you could spend the same $500 on an off-brand, trendy suit or dress that will be passé in a matter of two or three years.

Pay attention to quality and fit. Make sure that you love everything in your closet. If you put on something that makes you feel less than great, get rid of it. If you try on something in a store that can't be tailored to your body, don't buy it.

Personalize your look with accessories—high-quality shoes, scarves, bags, and jewelry that define your personal style.

Every time you get dressed, you should feel like you couldn't look any better even if money were no object. Making that happen is a big part of living rich.

Chapter 9

The Rich Man's Vacation

Traveling is one of the life's richest experiences. Few pastimes can provide such a combination of benefits—escape, adventure, relaxation, education. Even romance.

As with other topics covered in previous chapters, you don't need to spend a lot of money to travel "rich."

Disclosure: In discussing dressing like a billionaire, I admitted that I have no intuitive sense of style. In discussing travel, I should admit that I like to be pampered. I like to fly first class, stay at five-star hotels, be chauffeured to my destinations, and generally have my butt kissed. This kind of travel is—to be honest—wonderful and addictive. But it is also very expensive.

If it were up to me, I'd spend a fortune on travel because—well, because I can afford it. And if I did, I'd have very little to tell you about traveling rich on a budget. It so happens, however, that K is a very thrifty traveler. She refuses to pay rack rate for anything. When we travel together, we generally spend half of what I do on my own. And if she had her way, we'd spend even less. She simply can't get herself to fork out the big bucks for convenience. Instead, she spends a fair amount of time on the Internet searching for bargains. And she finds them.

Let's Talk About Luxury Travel

Luxury travel evokes images of catered safaris in African savannas, summer barge trips along European rivers, yacht charters down the coast of Turkey, or private viewings at art museums in Buenos Aires when they are closed to the public.

I've done all of those things. I've also hired a plane to fly K to Key West for an anniversary dinner… invited 15 of my best friends down to Nicaragua for an all-expense-paid golfing vacation… taken privately guided tours to amazing places in China, Cambodia, Thailand, Australia, Morocco, and a half-dozen European countries.

As I said above, I'm not going to pretend I didn't enjoy the expensive tours and vacations I've taken. Nor am I going to argue that certain aspects of traveling—flying first class versus coach, for example—are not simply better.

But if you were to ask me about my trips, I wouldn't be telling you, "Oh, the seats on our Virgin flight to London were so roomy!" Or, "We toured the city in the most comfortable Mercedes Benz."

My best memories of traveling are of looking at the sunset from a cliff high above the Irish Sea… rolling up to a pride of lions in the back of a pickup truck in Chad… sipping espresso in an Italian café… that sort of thing.

These are the richest experiences of traveling. And they aren't necessarily costly. Of the hundreds of meals I've eaten while traveling abroad, one of my favorites consisted of a baguette, a chunk of paté, and a bottle of *vin ordinaire* that K and I enjoyed in a small park on the right bank in Paris.

If I had to guess, I'd say that you could have all the fun and maybe 80 percent of the luxury of a $1,000-a-day trip for a third or even a quarter of that cost.

Let me give you an example. Right now, on my insistence, K and I are staying at Le Sirenuse, a five-star hotel in Positano, Italy. It is a very beautiful hotel, full of antiques and fresh flowers. We have, again at my insistence, booked a junior suite. The cost is $1,300 a day.

That is a hell of a lot of money.

This morning, to give me a reality check, K walked me into two adjacent hotels—a four-star hotel where rooms range from $300 to $400 a night and a charming three-star hotel where rooms range from $150 to $250. She wanted me to see those hotels so I could understand what she already knew—that the views from their terraces are every bit as good as the views from Le Sirenuse.

Last week, we were in Rome. There are plenty of famous restaurants in Rome where you can easily spend $250 per person. But there are also thousands of amazingly good trattorias where you can eat just as well for a tenth of the price.

Roman cuisine is actually very simple. And since Romans have an affinity for fresh foods and natural ingredients, it is very difficult to have a bad meal anywhere in the city, including the so-called tourist traps.

The point is that it makes no sense to spend a lot of money on fancy restaurants in Rome. You won't get a better meal. You'll get only the satisfaction of saying you've been there, whatever that's worth.

It Pays—Really Pays—to Do Lots of Research

As I said, K is the travel planner in our family. She seems to like the job because she spends (and I don't think I'm exaggerating) about as much time researching and booking our trips as we spend on them. But the results are terrific. We have first-class experiences for pennies on the dollar.

She likes boutique hotels with smaller rooms but elegant amenities. My main requirement is to have a bar and an outside terrace where I can smoke my cigars. (The latter is becoming increasingly difficult to find these days, so lately she's been finding hotels a block or two from a cigar bar.)

Her selections, I must say, are unerring. And the rates we pay are no more than a third of what I pay for a room at the Ritz when I do my business travel.

She often books us into hotels prior to their official openings. This means reduced prices and a staff that is trying very hard to please despite some inevitable glitches. By being willing to put up with these minor hiccups, we have been able to stay at some very chic hotels that she wouldn't consider later on because of their high cost.

K does her research on the Internet. But I notice that she also spends a good deal of time on the phone, interviewing clerks and concierges about accommodations, amenities, nearby restaurants, and points of interest. She also is an avid reader of the *New York Times* travel section, the *Hideaway Report* newsletter, and countless travel websites and books.

When you travel with K, you can be sure that the theater ticket you are holding has been purchased at half price, that the restaurant you are eating in has been highly rated, and that you are at least aware of what is "happening" in town even if you decide to pass. Before she even arrives at a destination, she has compiled a long list of art shows, cultural expositions, book readings, etc. that are often free to the public.

K much prefers subways to taxis and walking to subways. This— and her habit of reading about wherever we are—gives her an astonishingly good understanding of new towns and cities in the shortest possible time.

Invariably, our breakfast is included in the price of the room. And although I can sometime persuade her to have lunch or dinner at our hotel, she much prefers to go (i.e., walk) to some interesting place she has come upon in her research.

Often there is a bottle of wine and a bowl of fruit waiting for us when we check into a hotel for an extended stay. This, for K, is a perfect low-cost and healthy meal.

We can afford to do anything we want when we travel. But K has taught me that "traveling rich" is often a choice between spending money to do things impulsively and spending time to shop for value. The trick is to avoid doing the foolish things most wealthy people do—such as dining in the most famous restaurants—and find equally good experiences for a fraction of the price.

What About Travel Agents?

Despite the proliferation of online options, there has been resurgence in the use of travel agents. And, sometimes, it makes sense.

Travel agents have a wide network of connections. They know the execs at top hotels, cruise lines, and restaurants, and they have an insider's view of the way the industry works. If, for example, the 800 number you call says the hotel you were hoping to get is booked, chances are a good travel agent can access one of the rooms that are being held "just in case someone important needs it."

But let's be clear. The value of a travel agent increases in direct proportion to the cost and specialized components of your trip.

There are travel deals to be had every day. And many excellent websites keep making it easier to find deals tailored to your particular needs and budget. As a result, most of the time, you'll do even better on your own.

Recently, for example, I found the following deals online:

[bullet] A "European Extravaganza" featuring a 7-night European Cruise, starting at $589 per person; included up to $400 to spend on board A 7-night cruise on Royal Caribbean, starting at $749 Four-star Ft. Lauderdale beach hotels for up to 50 percent off Hawaii—3 nights, including airfare, hotel, and car rental—starting at $509

Not bad, right? Especially when you consider that this was the first time I tried to do this.

Value-Based Travel in the 21st Century

For booking a trip, K tells me your best bet is probably the old standbys: Orbitz, Expedia, Hotwire, Travelocity, and Kayak. But on the Internet, there's always something new… and sometimes better.

- **Hipmunk.com** was described by *Forbes* magazine as smarter, slicker, and quicker. A Hipmunk search is a "decision-making engine," fast and to the point. You get a timetable with colored bars ranked in descending order of "agony," a factor that includes price, length of trip, number of stops, and departure/arrival times.

- **Trippy.com** takes advantage of social networking by letting your globetrotting friends help you plan your vacation. Through Facebook, for instance, your online network can make recommendations that are automatically converted into an itinerary and plotted on a map.

- **TripIt.com** uses the latest technology to turn your flight, hotel, and car rental confirmation emails into a master itinerary.

Many useful sites have undoubtedly cropped up since I researched this. (You'll have to find them on your own.)

For the Ultimate in Cost-Saving: Couch Surfing

Couch surfing originally referred to "crashing" on the couch at friends' houses while traveling. Now, thanks to the Internet, it has evolved into an opportunity for everyone to experience another culture firsthand—not just people with friends in interesting places.

Through CouchSurfing.org and GlobalFreeLoaders.com, you can choose your location and get connected with people who live there and would be happy to put you up in their homes (and possibly act as your tour guide).

A notch above CouchSurfing.org and GlobalFreeLoaders is Airbnb.com. For a very modest fee, it books everything from city apartments to country villas in more than 34,000 cities and 190 countries.

To date, Airbnb has booked more than 10,000,000 rooms. According to a TechCrunch post, "On any given night in New York there are more people staying in homes via Airbnb than there are rooms in the biggest hotel in Manhattan."

10 Quick Money-Saving Tips

1. Flexibility pays off. If you can be flexible on when you travel (next week or three weeks later) and on which day you leave and return, you can save money.

2. Generally, it is cheaper to fly Tuesday, Wednesday, or Saturday.

3. Check a variety of airports. You may have cheaper options within a reasonable distance.

4. Some people are better than others at finding ways to collect and use frequent flyer miles. You'll find unbiased information on a forum called FlyerTalk.

5. If you subscribe to a frequent flyer program, sign up for promo codes. Promo codes can lead to savings of 10 to 50 percent.

6. Keep in touch with airlines via social networking. They have been known to tweet amazing deals.

7. You can bargain with a hotel for your room rate. Sixteen students at Columbia University did this as part of a research project—and every one of them got a discount, anywhere from 5 to 32 percent.

8. Hotel loyalty programs reward patrons with free nights, discounts, and special privileges. And those rewards can be used at any of the hotels in the chain. For instance, Hilton has ten distinct brands, including Waldorf Astoria, Conrad Hotels, DoubleTree, Embassy Suites, Garden Inn, Hampton Inn, and Homewood Suites.

9. You can book a room at up to 60 percent off if you are willing to do it through an opaque site such as Hotwire, Travelocity's Top Secret Hotels, or Priceline. The only catch is that you will not know which hotel you have booked until after you have paid. Consumer advocates have tried every trick in the book to match prices from these three sites with no luck.

10. Sign up for as many travel website emails as possible.

Beware of Hidden Hotel Fees

Before you book a hotel, read the fine print. Here are some of the traps to look out for:

- If a hotel offers golf, tennis, or hiking trails, they may add between $20 and $50 per day to your bill—whether you use the amenities or not.

- If you use the mini-bar, you may incur a "restocking" fee of $2.50 to $6 on top of the excessive cost of the snacks and drinks.

- Extra fees for early check-in and late departure have been increasing. And if you do arrive early or leave late and need to store your luggage, be prepared to pay per bag. (Such fees can often be waived if you're in the hotel's loyalty program.)

- Make sure you understand the hotel's cancellation policy. Some have increased the time from twenty-four hours to seventy-two.

- Room service may have a mandatory 18 percent tip added, in addition to the $2.50 to $5 service fee.

- You may have to pay to send a fax or access Wi-Fi.

No Matter How Much You Spend, Stress-Free Travel Means Planning Ahead

- Do your research. Know everything you can about your destination. You don't want to be surprised by unexpected weather, rules and regulations, exchange rates, or arrival/departure taxes.

- Prepare a list of emergency information that you can leave with someone back home. This should include your itinerary, as well as contact names/numbers for every place where you will be staying.

- Make sure that you have all required immunizations.

- Get your passport and visas organized a few months before your trip. To avoid potential red tape, check the requirements for each country you will be visiting.

- Buy a small notebook to take with you. On the first page, list the addresses of friends you may want to write to while you're away.

- Make copies of your travel documents, credit cards, and ID. Plan to tuck those copies away in your luggage… just in case.

- Take the correct currency with you. Traveler's checks are not welcome everywhere, and access to banks may be limited.

- If you are going to rent a car, make sure that your driver's license will be valid.

- If you are on prescription medication, take enough with you to cover unexpected travel delays.

- Look into getting travel medical insurance. If you already have a policy, review the fine print.

- Don't overpack. Put the clothes you think you will need in a neat pile—then remove 50 percent of them. This is easy to do if you keep your wardrobe simple. Just two colors and two or three pairs of shoes.

- A very good reason to keep your baggage to a minimum (aside from not having to lug around a lot of unnecessary stuff): Some airlines will hit you hard for the privilege of taking an extra piece of luggage.

- Don't expect American levels of service if you are traveling off the beaten path. Sometimes adventure and charm is more important.

- It may seem "touristy," but consider hiring a guide or booking a bus tour. It can help you ferret out the hidden gems in a city.

Chapter 10

The High Cost of Buying Prestige

I know people—doctors and lawyers and businesspeople—who make a lot of money. And they spend a lot of money.

When they buy a car, they opt for the most expensive one they can get. When they buy a home, they want the biggest one in the neighborhood. They wear Gucci shoes and carry Prada bags. All of their clothes and personal belongings must be recognizable upscale brands. And many go into serious debt to possess these symbols of wealth, becoming stressed-out slaves to the idols they worship.

In short, they are prestige junkies. And like all junkies, they are always looking for the next fix. The thrill of buying a $600 pair of shoes fades and is replaced by a yearning to buy a $700 pair. There is always an insatiable hunger for more.

And the irony is that the status they believe they are buying with brand names and big toys is often not delivered—or, if delivered, experienced for only a moment or two.

It irks me to see friends and colleagues spending their money this way. I don't like dining with them because they invariably prefer overpriced yet not-all-that-good restaurants simply because they are "the place to go." It saddens me to see their McMansions because they are huge and impersonal. They have been designed and furnished by professionals. They look and feel like hotels. Taking a tour of one of them inspires two questions: "How much did that cost?" And, "Who was your designer?" These are not the sort of questions you want people asking when they see your home.

I don't even like being in their cars. Not because expensive cars aren't good cars but because these people don't have the faintest appreciation of what a quality car should be. They don't know engines. They don't know suspension systems. They don't know braking systems. They just don't know.

But most of all, I don't enjoy listening to them talk about their *things* because, lacking the content of thought, they utter advertising-driven banalities.

So that is one fervent I hope that I have for this book: that I will convince you *not to be like them.*

Living rich is about making choices that improve the quality of your life—even if you don't have a ton of money. It's partly about understanding your choices and making smart spending decisions. But there's more to the experience of living rich than material things. Which brings me to Part II of this book…

Part II

Developing a Rich Mind

Chapter 11

The Most Important Thing I Ever Learned About Living Rich

It was about fifteen years ago. Jeff and I were having one of our long, luxurious lunches at a small Italian restaurant in Palm Beach. I was talking about one of the books I was writing at the time. I believe it was the first book I wrote as Michael Masterson: *Automatic Wealth*.

I admitted to him that I had been struggling with a definition for wealth. Jeff listened attentively (as he always did), complimented me on my thinking (as he always did), and asked, "What do you think of when you think of wealth?"

Among other things, Jeff was a master of the Socratic dialogue. I knew this question was just the first step of an intellectual walk I would be taking with him on the subject. I gamely went along.

"I'm not sure," I said. "That's what I'm trying to figure out."

"You are struggling to find a useful, abstract definition," he said. "An admirable goal. But that's not my question. I'm asking you what images arise when you think the word *wealth*?"

I closed my eyes. "Big houses with swimming pools and fancy cars," I said. "The usual symbols of wealth."

"Very good," he replied, Socratically. "Now imagine yourself lying on a lounge chair next to a swimming pool behind a big house with a fancy sports car parked in front."

Again, I closed my eyes.

"Do you have yourself in the picture?" Jeff asked.

"Yes," I told him.

"And how do you feel?" he asked.

"I don't know," I said. "Good."

"Can you be more precise?"

I focused on the feeling. "Tranquil," I said. "And safe."

At that point, we were interrupted by the waiter, and the conversation shifted to other things. But I was intrigued by the direction it had taken.

The initial images that the word *wealth* had brought to mind—big houses and pools and fancy cars—were very different from the feelings it evoked. Safety and tranquility? Really?

About a month later, Jeff and I had lunch again at the same restaurant. When I arrived, he was seated at our usual table, chatting with Giuseppe, the maître d'. He stood to greet me, then sat down and offered me a glass of Prosecco from the bottle that was chilling in front of him.

We enjoyed our meal and then carried what was left of the Prosecco to the patio. As always, every part of the meal with Jeff was slow, precise, and deliberate. He talked with interest about the menu. He sipped the wine with attentiveness. Time slowed down.

Our prior discussion about wealth hadn't come up during the meal, but I had been thinking about it. So I brought it up.

"I've been thinking about the conversation we had last month, about how I feel when I think about wealth," I told him. "And I see a connection between those feelings and the feelings I associated with poverty when I was a child."

As Jeff well knew, I grew up in a family of ten living on a teacher's income. We were the poorest people on Maple Avenue, which was one of the least desirable streets in town.

"Tell me about those feelings," he said.

"It was a combination of anxiety, the fear that my schoolmates would make fun of me for being poor… and insecurity, embarrassment because of the clothes I wore, the cheap bologna sandwiches I brought for lunch. That sort of thing," I said.

"So what's the connection between those feelings and your adult feelings about wealth?" he asked.

"Well," I said, "Seems to me that the safety and tranquility I now associate with wealth are the obverse of the insecurity and anxiety I associated with poverty as a child."

"That's an interesting observation," he said.

He paused and took a sip of wine. Then he asked, "How much time have you spent working to make money to buy the symbols you associate with wealth?" he asked.

"Lots of time," I admitted.

"Yet you found that when you had the money and the house and the cars, you still didn't have the feeling of being rich?"

"I'm not sure I know what you mean by that," I confessed.

He nodded and said, "Let's take a walk."

Digesting the Feeling of Richness

We took a walk along Worth Avenue and stopped at a small newsstand. "They have a great selection of international magazines," Jeff told me.

We spent some time looking through French and Italian and Chinese magazines that I had never seen before. As with lunch, the pace was leisurely, almost languid. The magazines I was looking at gave me ideas for improving some of the magazines I published. They gave me ideas about art projects I might start. I bought several that had especially inspired me. The cost was less than $20. And as we continued our walk, I found myself filled with energy and optimism.

This, I realized, was what Jeff meant by "feeling rich." Not the giddy, ephemeral feeling I got from spending lots of money on expensive "things," but this more subtle and enduring sensation.

It got me thinking. Here I was, already wealthy by any ordinary definition, and I was still spending most of my waking hours pushing myself forward on the endless path of making more money. I was doing it because I believed that this megalomaniacal effort would one day give me the *feeling* of being rich. But the emotions I was actually feeling were anxiety, anger, and sometimes depression.

Meanwhile, Jeff was doing something completely different. He had walked away from a $500,000 income (working with me in a previous life). He had slowed down and refocused his attention. And he seemed to be always tranquil and secure. In other words, he was feeling the emotions I wanted to feel but seldom did.

I don't want to misrepresent Jeff. He did not eschew the material things that money can buy. He enjoyed beautiful things and elegant service as much as I did. But he understood something that I didn't (and most people don't). He understood that it is not the things themselves that give you the feeling you are looking for. And by forcing me to slow down and pay close attention to aspects of the world around me that I would otherwise have ignored (like the magazines at that newsstand), he was teaching me what I needed to learn.

Nailing Down the Feeling

You need money—sometimes lots of money—to own the symbols of wealth. But to get the feeling of being *rich*, Jeff taught me that you don't need to spend much at all. In fact (and this is important),

I have found that owning things often diminishes the enjoyment I derive from them.

Let me give you an example. K and I used to buy season tickets to Miami Heat games. For many years, we sat courtside with other wealthy people, rooting for our team. The tickets came with many benefits: a VIP entrance, access to the VIP restaurant and players' lounge, invitations to private events, etc. It made us feel really special. But before long, I began to dread the hour-long ride to and from each game. Hiring a driver didn't help. It was the commitment of time. We started to give some of our tickets to friends. Eventually, we were making only a handful of games a season.

One year, because of scheduling issues (mostly related to my crazy workload) we made it to only three games. The cost of our tickets, including the playoffs, was something like $30,000. (It is higher now.) So that year, we were paying, in effect, $10,000 per game. That's insane, don't you think?

I realized that I should focus on the quality of the experience, not the idiotic snob appeal of being able to say that I was a season ticket holder. And it was clear that we could have a much better Miami Heat experience if we cancelled our season tickets and went to just a small number of really good games, paying for them ad hoc. We could get front row tickets from a scalper and have a leisurely overnight stay in a luxury hotel for about $1,500. Since then, we have a "Heat night" two or three times a year at a cost of $3,000 to $4,500. Just a fraction of what we were paying before… for a much better experience.

Another example. I once bought a small fishing boat for about $50,000—and I don't especially like fishing. It was an impulse buy. Not surprisingly, I took that boat out only once. For a fraction of what I paid for it, I could have rented a much bigger boat and invited a dozen friends to enjoy a day at sea. I would have saved a lot of money—and aggravation—and all of us would have had a memorable time.

It might make sense for a guy who truly loves fishing to buy a $50,000 boat. He'd use it all the time. For him, the "cost of use" each time he took the boat out would be minimal. And he would get a great deal of pleasure from his investment. But for me, owning a fishing boat was nothing more than owning a symbol of wealth.

When I make buying decisions now, I make an effort to focus on the feeling I am looking for—the feeling of richness—not the prestige I believe the purchase will provide. I remind myself that the "rush" of spending a lot of money lasts only a few moments, whereas the feeling of richness can be had in other ways while spending a great deal less.

For me, that feeling is a combination of three things. Not just the tranquility and safety I missed as a child, but also a sense of enrichment.

I get the feeling of tranquility by slowing down…

I get the feeling of safety by spending less than I can afford…

I get the feeling of enrichment by selecting experiences that add something to my life…

And what I have discovered is that when you focus on the feelings of wealth, you arrive at the desire for experiences, not things. That is the subject of the next chapter.

Chapter 12

Buying Happiness

In Part I of this book, we explored many ways to live rich on a budget. We talked about some big expenses, such as owning a house and a car. But we also covered other less costly things, such as clothing, food, drink, and even beds and vacations.

The claim I made over and over again is simple: It is possible to enjoy the best things in life for a fraction of the money that multimillionaires and billionaires spend on the same quality products and services.

This, it seems to me, is an incontestable good. Only a devout ascetic or a lunatic (there is no difference in my mind) could disagree.

To live rich in this way, you must understand and embrace two concepts:

The first concept—"cost of use"—was explained in Chapter 2 and applied in subsequent chapters. In a nutshell, there are smart and dumb ways to enjoy the best things in life. By paying only for the use you are likely to get from any thing or experience (a car, a house, a vacation), you can have it for a fraction of what it would cost you otherwise.

The second concept was explained in bits and pieces: When you buy a luxury good, a large part of what you are buying is the prestige of owning it. It is sometimes as much as 90 percent of the cost. And I believe you shouldn't pay for prestige. Not because prestige doesn't matter, but because it cannot be bought. All you can buy with a brand name is envy, jealousy, and unspoken resentment—none of which is worth a nickel.

Without understanding and accepting these two concepts, you can't live rich. Your experience of luxury will be limited by the limitations of your wealth and emotional intelligence. (Both, let's face it, are always limited.) You will either settle for second-rate products by buying when you should be renting (cost of use), or you will pay a fortune for prestige and realize later that you got nothing for it.

"Things" vs. Experiences: A Lot of Data Leading to an Interesting Conclusion

All of the topics covered in Part I concerned material things—houses, cars, mattresses, etc. And when it comes to living rich, material things do matter. A lot. There's no denying that they can make you happy. But there is good reason to believe that they will not bring you nearly as much happiness as you imagine.

I read a book recently that made this case. It's called *Happy Money*. Its authors, Elizabeth Dunn and Michael Norton, compare spending $200,000 on a house with spending the same amount of money on a flight into outer space. On the face of it, spending two hundred grand on a six-minute space flight might seem crazy. And even more crazy if you aren't wealthy and could have bought a house with that money.

But research, they say, suggests this is not necessarily true. "Remarkably, there is almost no evidence that buying a home—or a newer, nicer home—increases happiness." Moreover, they argue that spending the money on the space trip would provide more long-term satisfaction.

How can that be?

"Between 1991 and 2007," Dunn and Norton tell us, "researchers tracked thousands of people in Germany who moved to a new house because there was something about their old house they didn't like. Immediately after settling into their new abodes these movers reported being much more satisfied with their new homes than they'd been with their old ones."

As time passed, satisfaction with the new house did not diminish all that much. But what was remarkable was that the purchase of a new home did nothing at all to increase their satisfaction with their lives. "Their overall happiness didn't improve at all."

In another study, researchers found that a group of Harvard students that were lucky enough to get rooms in the dorms they wanted were no happier with their overall school experience than students who had to settle for lodging they initially didn't like.

And as recently as 2011, 90 percent of Americans said they believed home ownership to be a "central component of the America dream." Yet in study after study, home ownership does not seem to correlate to happiness.

To explain what's going on here, Dunn and Norton cited a study in which participants were asked to perform the following mental exercise:

> *Think of purchases you've made with the goal of increasing your own happiness. Consider one purchase that was a material thing, a tangible object that you could keep, like a piece of jewelry or furniture, some clothing or a gadget. Now think about a purchase you made that gave you a life experience—perhaps a trip, a concert, or a special meal. If you are like most people, remembering the experience brings to mind friends and family, sights and smells.*

Fifty-seven percent of the participants said that the experiential purchase made them happier. And other studies show that even when people spend only a few dollars, they get more lasting pleasure from buying an experience as opposed to a thing.

Dunn and Norton's research also indicates that sometimes even an unpleasant experience can provide happiness afterwards. They cited studies where people on a trip reported that they were having a less than enjoyable time. But when asked about the trip later, they remembered it as good. And veterans often remember their wartime experiences nostalgically.

Nostalgia turns out to be a very beneficial emotion, some scientists say. It allows us to convert difficult times into positive memories. That helps us cope with tough times ahead. And this makes sense to me. I have several times competed in national grappling meets. My nervousness prior to the events and the actual experience of fighting was anything but fun. But I have drawn enormous pleasure from remembering and recounting those experiences.

This was also true of the challenge of climbing Mount Kilimanjaro. The experience itself was excruciating. Yet I enjoy the memory of it more with each passing year.

My two years in the Peace Corps was half pleasure and half pain. But thinking about it has provided me with a great deal of happiness over the thirty years since then.

It seems, then, that the actual pleasure you get from an experience is not the most important criteria for determining its ultimate value. You have to look at it from a long-term perspective.

Relative Values

Dunn and Norton make a convincing case for investing in expensive experiences instead of expensive things. Are they right?

Since I have no studies from which to draw conclusions, I will research my memory banks instead.

I remember, for example, that when I was in my thirties and forties I felt that money spent on vacations was largely wasted because the experience itself was finite. I thought it made much better sense to spend $10,000 on a used car or a handful of gold coins than on a family trip.

My good friend Eddie agreed with me. But his wife Barbra and my wife had a very different idea. They thought money spent on trips to Europe were good investments. And so we went. Year after year, for more than a decade.

Looking back now, I can see that they were right. I value those trips not just for the good times I remember but also for what I learned during our travels and (most especially) for how it deepened our friendship.

Another example. For more than twenty years, K and I have sponsored a sort of extended family reunion. We call it "Cousin Camp." We pick a destination where about forty of us congregate to have an adventure for several days or a week. These reunions have become increasingly expensive over the years. Nowadays, each one costs us considerably more than $100,000. My former self would have thought that it would have been smarter to invest that money in some tangible assets and perhaps divvy up those assets among those same people. But I don't feel that way. And neither, I think, do the family members that have been enjoying this experience.

Now let's look at the "things" I've bought.

On top of the list in terms of costliness is my house and my art collection and my two vacation residences. Then, much less costly, cars, jewelry, etc. Oh, and my cigars.

I must say that I enjoy all of these things very much.

Am I saying that Dunn and Norton are wrong? No. Because when I think about it, I realize that the great pleasure I get from these things comes from the *experience* of them.

The cars I most enjoyed, for example, were the old cars I restored and drove on special occasions. The reason I love my house so much is because it has been an ongoing project of restoration and improvements. Likewise, art for me is not just an investment. My art collection crowds every room I live and work in. I have spent countless hours enjoying those objects.

So I believe the argument that Dunn and Norton make in *Happy Money* is a solid one.

Things themselves, even those we most associate with happiness, aren't very good at delivering enduring satisfaction. It's the experiences we have that give us the most happiness over the long run.

What Can We Take From This?

First, that it is a mistake to think, as I did when I was a young man, that it is not smart to spend money on experiences because experiences end in a matter of days or weeks. In fact, the pleasure we derive from experiences can endure for years—even a lifetime.

Second, that even though experiences generally provide more satisfaction than things, you can get great and long-lasting pleasure from the things you love by turning them into experiences.

Chapter 13

Discovering Value and Purpose

To have a rich life, you need a rich mind. And the rich mind recognizes that spending money on things will not automatically add to its lifetime store of happiness. It prefers to spend money on meaningful experiences, recognizing that quite often very little money needs to be spent. But it also recognizes that when money is spent on a material object, that object can bring happiness if it is enjoyed over time.

Time is, in fact, a very important factor in living rich. It may be the one particular non-material aspect of life that matters more than anything else.

So let's talk about that now—how to make the time you spend *richer*. And let us begin with an activity that will likely consume the greatest amount of your time: the time you spend working.

Most people have a love/hate relationship with work. I know I did.

From the time I was a kid, it was something I *had* to do. And I hated that. At the same time, I loved the feeling of accomplishment when I did a good job. And, of course, I loved the money.

As the second of eight children, I was working around the house as soon as I could pick up a broom. At four, I was cleaning up my room. At six, I was drying the dishes. At nine, I was responsible for cleaning the bathrooms on Saturdays and washing the walls along the stairwell where my siblings were always leaving dirty fingerprints. And as soon as I was legally able to work part-time (at age 12), I had a paper route five mornings a week and I worked Saturday afternoons and Sundays at the local car wash.

I had to work because we were a big family living on a teacher's meager salary. Also because my parents believed that work was good. Now, I am grateful to them for that. But at the time, I didn't understand the benefit I was getting from it.

When I dreamed, I dreamed I was a rich kid who had a chauffeur who drove me to school in a white limousine. I wore a white tuxedo and sported a diamond-tipped cane. I dreamed of being rich because I was embarrassed by my family's relative poverty. We lived in a small house across from the municipal storage facility and electric plant. Our playground was the town's sandpit. We wore secondhand clothes donated by local charities.

What I didn't understand was that in many ways we had a very rich upbringing. My parents were educated and believed we should be educated too. At supper, my father would read to us from the Bible or from great works of literature. On Sunday mornings, my mother supervised us in memorizing poetry.

I paid my way through college by working all sorts of manual jobs. And I graduated debt free and *magna cum laude*. I went on to acquire a master's degree from the University of Michigan and an all-but-Ph.D. from Catholic University, funding my tuition with a pool installation business I started with some friends.

At 25, I was ready to take on the world. But instead of going into the workforce, I applied to become a Peace Corps volunteer and got accepted to a program teaching English literature at The University of Chad in Africa. This turned out to be an invaluably rich experience, although I was paid only $50 a week.

When I got out of the Peace Corps, I got a job as an editor of a newsletter in Washington, D.C., called *African Business & Trade*. I got the job because of my experience in Africa, which included writing for the Peace Corps newsletter and authoring a few small books on the side. I knew nothing about business, but I did the best I could to learn as much as I could. During that time, I wrote my first professionally published book, *Information Peking*, about doing business in China.

Eventually, I convinced my boss to let me take a stab at running the business. I have no idea why he allowed me to do it… but he did. After two years of trying and failing to increase sales, I was offered a position as editorial director of a fledgling publishing company in South Florida. A year into that job, I signed up for a fourteen-week course that I thought would help me become better at public speaking. (In my new job, I had to run staff meetings and give a lot of presentations.)

The course wasn't exactly what I expected. It was based on Dale Carnegie's book *How to Win Friends and Influence People*, and it was basically about setting and achieving goals.

The first week, we were given a challenge. We had to identify all the things we wanted to do with our lives, then narrow them down to one main goal.

This was hard for me. I wanted to be a teacher. I wanted to be an author. I wanted to paint. I wanted to be a martial artist and a world traveler and at least a dozen other things. I also wanted to be rich. That dream had never left me.

The following week, I was going to have to stand up and announce the one goal that would be my priority. The rest of the course would be devoted to taking the first steps toward making it happen.

Driving to class that day, I was in a panic. I had narrowed my goals to three: to be a teacher, an author, and a millionaire. How could I choose just one? That would mean giving up the other two!

Minutes before class began, I made my decision. My number one priority would be getting rich. I figured that if I could do that first, I would have the time and money to do anything else I wanted to do.

That decision changed my life.

I began to look at every choice I made and every action I took in terms of this one goal—asking myself whether it would enhance or take away from my prospects of gaining wealth. This was a radical change in my thinking and it had immediate and amazing effects.

Within weeks, I had talked my way into a promotion. In six months, I had doubled my yearly income. Before my thirty-fourth birthday, I was both a partner in a growing business and a bona fide millionaire. I had achieved my number one goal!

I continued working like mad. Over the next five years, my partner and I grew the business to well over a hundred million dollars. And then, suddenly, he had a heart attack and decided, almost overnight, that he wanted to retire.

We sold the business in pieces. I was thirty-nine years old and had a net worth in excess of $10 million. But I was also exhausted. So I decided to see what it would be like to live a life of leisure. I bought a warehouse that I converted into a "man cave," and I spent four hours a day there, writing short stories and painting. Afternoons I spent exercising, learning Brazilian Jiu Jitsu, and reading by the pool. And on weekends and holidays, I traveled with my family.

It was an exciting and enjoyable time. But it occurred to me that although I wasn't "working" anymore, I was still working. I began to think about what it was about "work" that I didn't like and why the four to six hours a day that I was putting into writing and Jiu Jitsu was so satisfying.

I realized that what gave me pleasure about writing and practicing Jiu Jitsu was not that it was fun (it was sometimes very difficult) and not that I didn't *have to* do it (I felt compelled to continue). But the work itself gave my life *purpose*. And the products of my work—the stories I was publishing and the skill I was developing on the mats—were things I *valued*.

This was a life-changing revelation. And it is one of the core ideas behind what we are talking about in this part of the book. It is one of the fundamental concepts that can help you have the life you want. It is a guiding principle that will enable you to spend your time *richly*.

Chapter 14

Life's Trickiest Trade-Off

Andy and Jack were best friends growing up in Chagrin Falls, Ohio. After graduating from high school, they both went to NYU and graduated with business degrees in 1972. Andy got a job as an investment analyst on Wall Street. Jack decided to return to Ohio to help his aging father run the family restaurant.

They agreed to meet up the following summer in Brazil for an adventure trip boating down the Amazon River. But when summer rolled around, they were both too busy to do it.

A year later, Jack had the restaurant running smoothly and was ready to go.

"I'd love to go," Andy said. "But I'm in the middle of an executive training program. "Maybe next year."

The following year, Andy couldn't go because he had just taken on a "big" client. The year after that, it was a new boss. Then it was a promotion. At his wedding, Andy swore to himself that he would definitely do the Amazon trip "in the next two years." Fifteen months later, he and his wife had their first child.

Jack kept in touch and would sometimes tease Andy about the trip.

"It's going to happen one of these days," Andy would say. "I promise."

At their fortieth high school reunion, Andy and Jack saw each other for the first time since they had graduated from NYU. Andy had become a very wealthy man and dressed the part. Jack had lived a comfortable, middle-class life.

That night in the high school parking lot, while their classmates danced to old music, Jack and Andy sat on a bicycle stand, sipping beer and looking toward the football stadium.

"So what's it really like?" Jack asked.

"What is *what* like?"

"You know—being a rich guy, on a day-to-day basis?"

Andy thought about it. "Well, I have lots of nice things. But the typical day for me is like this. I wake up early and force myself to work out because I know the moment I start working I'll be working for eleven hours straight. The work is challenging. On any typical day I am all over the map emotionally. I go from mild aggravation to moments of feeling very good about myself to bouts of anger, insult, shame, pride, humiliation, hope…"

"Sounds grueling."

"It is."

"But at least you have those nice things and the vacations."

Andy smiled.

"And how is it for you?"

"You mean what's it like being a poor guy?"

"You're not poor."

"No, I'm not poor. But I'm far from rich. In some ways I think I have a better life than you do. I get up and read the paper at breakfast. Then I piddle around in the basement, working on my little hobbies. At four, I go to the restaurant and stay there till about ten. Then I go home. I read or watch TV for a while and go to bed."

"You're right," said Andy. "That is a better life. I'm envious."

"But that's just part of the equation. We drive around in cheap little economy cars. We need a new roof but I don't have the money for it so I'm paying to have the leaks patched. We pay our bills but have no savings. We worry about helping our kids with their college tuition. And retirement? We haven't saved a penny."

Time and Money... Money and Time

Time and money. They do seem to be connected: We can spend our time earning money or we can spend our money enjoying our time.

The obstetrician can afford a four-week vacation in Honolulu but doesn't have the time to take it. The high school teacher has more than four weeks off every summer but can't afford that kind of trip.

The more time you devote to making money, the more money you are likely to make. But what good is that money if you have no time left to enjoy it?

It was Ben Franklin who said that time is money. What he actually said was: "Remember that time is money. He that can earn ten shillings a day by his labor, and goes abroad, or sits idle, one half of that day, though he spends but sixpence during his diversion or idleness… has really spent, or, rather, thrown away, five shillings besides."

Franklin was not saying that you should spend *no* time traveling or having fun (sitting idle). He was saying only that you should be aware of the financial cost of your time.

If you are a consultant and make $100 an hour, each day you spend away from work "costs" you $800. So when calculating the cost of a vacation, you must include that per-diem "expense."

Likewise, if you make $100 an hour… does it make sense to mow your own lawn? From a strictly financial perspective, it is foolish.

You "save" the $20 an hour a gardener would charge you but net out to a loss of $80 per hour.

Being aware of the monetary value of your time is a necessary part of making smart decisions about the time-versus-money tradeoff.

But it's only one part of the equation.

How Bill Spent His Weekends

For about six years, Bill Bonner and I shared the same office space. We were both busy doing the same work: growing a profitable international publishing company. On weekends, I would go home and continue working on the business. Bill would go to his farm and build walls out of stone.

Building stone walls is difficult and strenuous work. It is also very poorly paid work. Bill understood that he was working "far under his pay scale" on Saturdays. But he chose to do it because it gave him pleasure.

Bill also may have believed that he could do only so much high-quality brainwork in any given week. He may have believed that the manual labor he did on Saturday (and the idle time he spent on Sunday) recharged his business-building batteries somehow.

And he may have been right. The business grew from $8 million to $100 million in about four years, and then from $100 million to $500 million in the ten years that followed. Except for business travel, Bill never felt obliged to abandon his work/non-work schedule.

Mein Kampf

Over the years, my own struggle with the money/time quandary changed but did not abate. I often wondered…

- Why is it that I'm still working sixty hours a week when I don't need any more money?

- Why do I find it so difficult to stop thinking about work when I'm with my friends and family?

- Why is my weekly schedule jam-packed with work and hobby time? Why can't I give myself a half-day off without feeling guilty?

I still wonder whether I could have worked half the hours I worked in the past and made the same amount of money. I wonder what I could have gained in intimacy had I spent more time with my children. I wonder if my maniacal drive to become a more accomplished person affected my health.

What About You?

You may have these same questions. You may have others. All responsible people must ask themselves: "How much time should I spend earning money versus relaxing versus self-improvement versus taking care of family and friends?"

Let's begin with three simple observations.

Observation #1: We have inherent responsibilities.

When I asked my father why he abandoned his first career as a dramatist to become a college teacher, he told me that he felt his "primary moral responsibility" was to support his family. Teaching was not (and is not now) a well-paid profession. But it was enough to keep his wife and eight children clothed and fed. I admired him for that.

My mother was a contrarian thinker. A Catholic by upbringing, she was critical of the church and had progressive views of right and wrong. But she did leave her children with one old-fashioned idea about how to behave. She told us over and over that we should "leave the world a little bit better" than we found it.

And that is what I believe. Regardless of the circumstances we are born into, each of us is bound to earn the money needed to support his family and to leave the world a little better than he found it.

Observation #2: Being rich is better than being poor.

I was poor for thirty-three years. It was a good thirty-three years. Wouldn't trade it for anything, as they say. But I have also been rich for thirty years. And that, too, has been good.

I can't say that my overall happiness/equanimity/whatever has been greater in my rich years than it was in my poor years. But I can say that I am definitely happy that I got rich.

Now I might be happy about my wealth because, growing up poor, I needed the ego gratification of succeeding at life's most universal contest: making money. Had I been heir to a fortune, perhaps I wouldn't value wealth. Unless, of course, I lost it.

Observation #3: Work is sometimes fun and sometimes miserable.

I worked hard to become wealthy. Some of that work was fun. A lot of it was not.

You might think that the fun work was flying to exotic locations, meeting powerful people, and counting my money. And that the un-fun work was slaving away at some project till nine or ten o'clock at night. Or perhaps you think that the fun work was the work that resulted in financial windfalls while the un-fun work was the work that resulted in losses.

None of that was true. The fun I took from traveling and hobnobbing evaporated rather quickly. And the fun I had in earning a $5,000 bonus disappeared immediately, only to be recaptured by a bonus twice that size.

In retrospect, I understand the factors involved in what made work fun. Working on projects I valued was the most important factor. Doing good work on a project I valued (work I knew to be good) was a close second.

From 1982 to 1993, I earned millions of dollars every year and acquired an eight-figure fortune. But I never truly valued the work I was doing then, so the amount of "fun" time I had while working was limited.

Since 1994, the fun I get out of work has been steadily increasing. That is a direct result of a gradual increase in the time I spend working on projects I value. I am talking about my charitable activities (for which I do not make but contribute money). But I am also talking about the books I write and some of the businesses I work with.

Two Secrets for Finding Happiness in Work

If you are not born rich, you must work to make money. How much time you devote to making money depends on whether you feel, as I do, responsible for the financial welfare of your family and whether you believe you should leave the world a little better than you found it.

If you feel that way, you will almost certainly have to work at least forty hours a week. If your financial ambitions are more than getting by, you will have to work fifty to sixty hours a week for a good many years.

But if you can learn to enjoy the time you spend making money, your life will be that much richer. You won't have to fill up your happiness piggybank outside of work. You will be able to get much or even most of your happiness from the time you spend working.

This leads to my first recommendation: If you possibly can, you should find a way to make money by doing something you believe is valuable. And if you don't have that luxury right now, you should gradually move your career in that direction.

You should also recognize that having a career that you value is just one part of a two-part process. You must also do work that is clearly good. Work that has purpose.

And this leads to my second recommendation: Never work like you don't like your work. Work hard. Work carefully. Work like it matters.

Finding the Optimal Balance

This hardly completes our inquiry into time and money. Nor does it fully answer the question posed by the story about Jack and Andy that I told you at the beginning of this chapter.

To live a rich life, you must find pleasure in your work. But you must also find pleasure outside work. With your friends and family and community and in your personal pursuits and education.

How much time should you devote to those other obligations and activities?

It might be helpful to think of the time you spend in terms of four major categories: your wealth, your health, your social time, and your personal time.

• Your wealth

A typical workweek for a person who is serious about acquiring wealth is between forty and sixty hours. Let's settle on fifty hours.

• Your health

There is no question that sleeping and exercise are two of the most important—and time-consuming—factors in good health. Sleep experts recommend seven to eight hours a night. Let's round that down to fifty hours a week. Some people like to exercise several hours a day. But the latest studies show that for health purposes thirty minutes per day of intense exercise is all that is needed. A half-hour a day is three-and-a-half hours a week. Let's round that up to five hours.

So far we have fifty hours a week devoted to your wealth and fifty-five hours devoted to your health.

We are left with social time and personal time. And we are left with sixty-three hours (24 hours x 7 days = 168 hours – 105 hours = 63 hours). That's nine hours a day.

• Your social time and personal time

The amount of time you spend socially (with family, friends, and community) versus the time you spend personally (learning, developing skills, practicing hobbies, relaxing, playing games, etc.) is a matter of circumstance.

When you have a young family, you will be spending most of those sixty-three hours socially. (With your kids or escaping them.) As an empty nester, you'll be able to spend more of those hours on personal interests.

All of this suggests that the twenty-four hours each of us has in a given each day is sufficient to make the money we need, stay fit and healthy, have a fulfilling social life, and develop our personal interests.

So the next time you find yourself thinking, "There is never enough time," remind yourself that there *is* enough time. You have enough hours. But you may not be optimizing them. When you optimize your time, you will be able to accomplish all you need to without feeling worn down. On the contrary, you will feel energized throughout your entire day.

Chapter 15

Life-Enriching Choices

From the perspective of living rich, there are three kinds of experiences. There are experiences that:

1. Improve you somehow

2. Leave you more or less the same

3. Damage or diminish you in some way

Look at almost any activity and you will see what I'm talking about.

On your commute to work, for example, you have a fair amount of "free" time. You can spend that time getting aggravated about traffic, laughing at idiotic conversations on talk radio, or listening to an audiotape on some subject you care about—maybe a lesson on speaking a foreign language.

Getting apoplectic about the dimwit in front of you who's driving with his turn signal on will harm you. It will upset you. It will drain your energy. And that will make you less capable of doing good work when you arrive at the office.

Listening to talk radio may amuse you. And if it does, time will pass quickly. That can feel like a benefit if you view your commute as time to kill. But killing time is never a good idea unless you are in pain.

Spending your commute listening to and repeating Spanish phrases might not sound like a lot of fun. But if learning Spanish is a goal of yours, you will certainly feel better about yourself by the time you arrive at work.

You see what I mean. When it comes to our free time, we have choices: spend it wisely, wastefully, or self-destructively. Choose one.

We have these three options every minute of every day—except perhaps when we are sleeping. That amounts to 960 choices (sixteen hours times sixty minutes) a day.

Free time, of course, does not present itself in discrete minute-by-minute blocks. But there are still many, many choices. The average person spends four to six hours a day watching TV or amusing himself with video games. Add to that commuting time, time spent sitting around waiting for something to happen, time spent doing stupid things you don't have to do… it adds up quickly. Even four wasted hours a day equals twenty-eight hours a week or more than 2,000 hours a year. That is enough time to write a book, compose a symphony, build a cottage, or acquire competency in any two complex skills (e.g., playing a musical instrument, speaking a foreign language, becoming a public speaker, learning how to write advertising copy, etc.).

Time is a limited and very precious commodity. You cannot ignore it. You cannot pretend it doesn't matter. You have to accept your responsibility for every minute of it and decide: Will you kill it? Use it to kill you? Or invest in it to make your life richer?

I starting thinking (and writing) about this fifteen years ago. Since then, I've tried repeatedly to make good choices. It isn't easy (for reasons I'll explain in a moment). But one thing that has helped me make decisions was to name my options.

The idea: If I am going to make a bad choice, at least I should have the courage to call it bad.

The Three Choices

• **Self-Destructive Habits**

I tell people who don't know me that I never met a self-destructive habit I didn't like. If you aren't attracted to self-destruction, you have no idea what I'm talking about. Or maybe you have self-destructive habits but refuse to recognize them. A self-destructive habit is anything you do that makes you intellectually, morally, emotionally, or materially poorer.

Gorging on junk food is a self-destructive pastime. And however happy I have felt while I was doing it, I always felt that much worse afterwards. The same goes for drinking rum and getting into fights and lying and cheating. The criterion isn't how I feel at the time but how these things leave me feeling later on.

There are many behaviors that we might all agree are self-destructive. Some of those I've mentioned could be put on the list. But—legalities aside—the ultimate judgment about what is self-destructive is a personal one. We are, after all, talking about your mind. (And by mind, I include your heart.) Only you know whether a particular behavior makes you feel better or worse, healthier or sicker, richer or poorer.

• Zombie Behavior

There are many pleasant ways to kill time. Many, many more than there were when I was a kid. In my teenage years, television was a boring, black-and-white affair. Other than Saturday mornings, there was nothing on that little square box that was worthy of my attention. Nowadays, we all have an infinite number of options when it comes to amusing ourselves. But many—if not most—of those options don't do us any good.

They entertain us. They divert us. They pass the time. But they don't make us better in any way. In fact, studies have shown that extended TV watching puts our brains into a kind of zombie zone that lasts long after the TV is turned off.

I like my zombie pastimes. I like watching mixed martial arts, listening to Howard Stern, and playing solitaire. I like drinking tequila and smoking cigars. I like eating pasta. I like my zombie experiences especially when I am tired or sad or disappointed. They seem to beckon me, promising to soothe me. And they do, for a while. But after an hour (or four) of zombie time, I never feel better. I feel more or less the same but a little ashamed of myself.

• **Enriching Experiences**

Our third option is the obvious winner: choosing an activity that somehow improves you, leaving you feeling (or actually being) wiser, smarter, more understanding, happier, healthier, stronger, etc.

So why is it that we don't always choose enriching activities when deciding how to spend our free time?

The reason has to do with energy. Enriching activities take more of it. It takes more energy, for example, to practice my French horn than to play solitaire. I don't know why that is, but it is.

And if it requires, say, 100 units of mental energy to play the French horn for fifteen minutes, it takes 1,000 units to will myself to open up my case, blow the spit out of the valves, and put the mouthpiece to my lips. Again, I don't know why that is, but it is a fact of my life.

Another reason that we don't always choose enriching activities is because it is usually—and almost always initially—non-addictive. I've put at least forty hours into studying Italian, and so far have felt not a single impulse to continue. Each practice session requires willpower to initiate and energy to push through. I do think I know why that is. Practicing Italian is stressful for me because it is difficult. And it is difficult because I am not good at it.

Making the Right Choice:
The Five-Minute Trick

So we have three choices. And a hundred times a day, if we are conscious, we have the freedom to make wise or wasteful or self-destructive decisions. It is never a problem to know which of the options is the right one. The problem is summoning up the energy to make the right decision.

Driving to work, your energy stores may be low because you have not yet done anything active. Driving home from work, your energy stores may be depleted. Still, you are spending some amount of time in your car and you have a choice. You can listen to that Spanish language tape, you can listen to Howard Stern, or you can… I don't know, keep glancing at your odometer to see if you can catch it rolling over into the next set of multiple zeroes.

You know you should be doing the Spanish tape, but you just don't feel like it. So what do you do?

There are many answers to that question. But here's what I do when I find that I'm going to be stuck behind the wheel for a fairly long period of time. (I don't drive to work.) I make a deal with myself. Practice language for five minutes, I tell myself, and then you can listen to Howard Stern for the rest of the trip.

I have convinced myself that I can do anything for five minutes— even hold my head under water. (Four minutes and five seconds is my record.) So I do the five minutes. And most of the time, something marvelous happens. After about two minutes, my stress level drops considerably. After another minute or two, I find that I'm actually enjoying the work.

This doesn't happen all the time, but it happens most of the time. And so my five minutes of enrichment turns into ten minutes and then into fifteen minutes. Sometimes it lasts the entire trip.

As I said, I don't drive to work. So for me (and maybe you?), the challenge I face every morning is a little different. Still, I have to force myself to make choices that will get my brain in gear.

After breakfast, I head up to my office above the garage. I'm tempted to head right to my computer and read email… see what's come in overnight. But most email is zombie work. Ninety percent of it will not enrich you. Ninety percent of it will enrich other people or no one at all.

Doubtful? You can prove this to yourself objectively by looking at the last twenty emails you wrote and asking in every case, "Did this improve me?" Or you can decide subjectively by figuring out how you feel about email. If it feels easy to do almost to the point of being addictive, then it's zombie work.

I want to do email. So how do I overpower the zombie part of my brain? I make the same sort of deal with myself. I tell myself that before I do any email, I must first spend five minutes doing something enriching, like writing. In fact, I have no intention of spending just five minutes writing. My goal is to spend at least sixty minutes writing. But I get there by tricking myself with the five-minute promise, which turns into fifteen minutes and then into an hour. An hour is easy.

After writing for an hour, I feel pretty good about myself and I am usually full of energy. I will often keep writing then, sometimes for another hour, sometimes for two or three. But I have other things I need to accomplish besides writing. So I use an egg timer to limit my writing time to an hour. When the egg timer rings, I get up and do another productive thing, such as stretching or playing a brain game or practicing my French horn. Since I'm not trying to become a concert-level French horn player, I limit my practice to fifteen minutes. When I'm done with that, my energy stores are even higher. I use that extra energy to practice Italian (or French or Spanish or German—don't ask) for another fifteen minutes. By then I'm brimming with good feelings and still charged to the hilt and so I'll take on a challenging business task or go back to my writing.

This is what I do. And it works for me.

An enriching activity doesn't have to be practicing a musical instrument or learning a foreign language or writing poetry. It can be as simple as reading an inspiring or informative book. An enriching activity takes energy, as I said, but it gives you back that energy and more for your time invested. And it makes you feel like a better version of who you are or who you want to be.

A Cheat Sheet for How to Spend Your Time

Following is a list I jotted down—a list of what are, for me, enriching ways to spend my time. These correspond to my personal value system. You may have different ideas for the sort of activities that are likely to leave you feeling like a better version of yourself.

My enriching activities include:

- Reading inspirational or informative material

- Drawing and/or painting

- Writing fiction, nonfiction, poetry, essays, etc.

- Practicing Brazilian Jiu Jitsu

- Engaging in demanding physical exercise

- Watching educational documentaries

- Listening to uplifting music

- Paying attention to fine art

- Watching a really, really good movie

- Having a good conversation with a thoughtful person

My zombie activities include:

- Reading crime fiction

- Playing solitaire

- Watching TV shows like "Justified" and "Downton Abbey"

- 90 percent of the email I do

- Drinking and socializing (As Ernest Hemingway once said, "I drink to make other people more interesting.")

My self-destructive activities include:

- Drinking too much and saying things I regret the next day

- Gossiping

- Fighting (for any reason)

- Watching reality TV

- Other things I'd rather not talk about right now

You may not agree with some of my choices. That's okay. You can (and should) make your own list. But in creating that list, consider the following:

Making enriching choices...

- Teaches you something worth knowing or develops a skill worth having

- Fosters an understanding of people and situations you had been previously closed to

- Strengthens you spiritually, intellectually, and emotionally

- Builds confidence and develops your ability to make wise choices in the future

- Is hard to do—until you get good at it

- Leaves you feeling energized

Making zombie choices...

- Teaches you nothing

- Requires no thought

It is watching TV rather than going to a stage play. It is getting a massage rather than practicing yoga. It is chugging a brewski rather than savoring a good wine.

- Tends to be habit-forming

Because it feels good (in a medium-energy sort of way) and is so easy to do, you find yourself doing it over and over again.

- Is easy and as comfortable as an old pair of slippers

Zombie choices are tried-and-true diversions that pass the time.

- Leaves you with the unpleasant feeling that you've wasted your time

Making self-destructive choices...

- Feels really good at the beginning

- Attracts bad company

Since most smart people don't approve of what you are doing, you find yourself doing it with another set of friends. Eventually, you reject the people who "don't get it." They are too straitlaced or lame to understand, so you figure you don't need them in your life.

- Disables you intellectually, emotionally, and physically

You become less capable of performing complex skills or dealing with complex issues. Eventually, you are less capable of peak performance overall.

- Is more than habit-forming, it is addictive

Self-destructive activities have ever-extending thresholds. What gets you off in the beginning is never enough to get you off later on. You mistakenly believe that more is always better.

- Leaves you feeling like a failure

When we are at our best—confident and full of energy—enriching activities are an easy choice. When we are feeling just okay, we can usually reject self-destructive pastimes but tend toward zombie activities. And when we are at our worst—low in energy and full of doubt—we are most susceptible to self-destructive choices.

But you can make good choices.

Five Steps to Making the Right Choice

1. Identify the experiences that are, for you, enriching, zombie, and self-destructive. Make a list like the one I made above.

2. Pay attention to time—all the time. Assess the amount of time you typically spend each day on enriching, zombie, and self-destructive activities.

3. Make a commitment to change.

4. Accomplish that transformation by making little "deals" with yourself. Before you engage in a self-destructive or zombie activity, force yourself to spend at least five minutes doing something that leaves you richer.

5. Build from there.

Chapter 16

Richness From Art

If you want to live a rich life, you shouldn't ignore the many pleasures art can provide.

I'm talking about visual art—painting, drawing, and sculpture. Also handcrafted, utilitarian objects—pottery, rugs, furniture, and ceramics.

Like literature, art can make statements and tell stories. Like music, art can stir up thoughts and feelings without language or logic. And like dance, art can inspire us and elevate our very notion of beauty.

I've been arguing that having a rich mind is about spending your leisure time profitably. It's about getting a high emotional and intellectual return on your hobbies—without spending a lot of money doing so.

Many think of art appreciation as a diversion for the rich and the well-educated. In fact, it is a very democratic pastime.

You don't need money to appreciate art. You simply need the ability to look at it. The street sweeper in Florence, Italy, has the same capacity as the CEO of Ferrari to enjoy Michelangelo's famous sculpture, *David*. The laborer cutting grass on the Florida millionaire's estate has the same capacity as the estate owner to admire the Fernando Botero sculpture sitting in that very garden.

Wealth can actually be a hindrance to the enjoyment of art. I know more than a handful of wealthy people who buy art and pretend to enjoy it. They believe it gives them prestige. They fill their homes with "limited editions" from well-known artists, such as Salvador

Dali and Marc Chagall. To that same end, they fill their garages with Porsches and Lamborghinis. I sometimes wonder if—aside from showing off their trophies to visitors—they ever even look at them.

Just as you don't need money to appreciate art, you don't need a specialized education. Having a college degree, even a graduate degree in art history, might help you talk impressively about art. It might provide you with the vocabulary to describe the technical aspects of a piece or explain its historical context. But it doesn't give you an advantage when it comes to really seeing art or enjoying it in a personally enriching way.

I have many friends who "know" about art and are happy to talk about it. They attend the must-see exhibitions. They favor the fads. And when touring a museum, they're interested only in the featured works of the best-known artists.

A true art lover doesn't act that way. He looks at a lot of art. He can't stop himself from looking at art. He has his own ideas and preferences based on his own personal experience.

How to Deepen Your Experience of Art

I was in grammar school when I first began looking at art with interest. At that time, I liked painted clowns on black velvet better than I liked Rembrandt. I like Rembrandt better now, but I don't think it's because I've taken a few art classes and read a few dozen books. I think it's because I have spent so much time looking.

The pleasure I got from looking at those clown paintings was real and valid. But it was a simple pleasure—sort of like the pleasure I got from drinking sweet wines when I first began to drink wine.

As time passed, those clown paintings seemed less interesting to me. I didn't want them to. It simply happened. It happened—I think—because I was seeing so much other art.

There seems to be a natural evolutionary process that takes place when you expose yourself to any of life's aesthetic pleasures—art, music, dance, literature, food, or wine. In the early stages, you tend to like the simple and obvious. Later on, you prefer the subtle and complex.

I am not saying that there's anything wrong with the simple and obvious. I'm saying that if you devote time to any aesthetic endeavor, you should almost always expect your tastes to mature in the direction of subtle and complex.

This may sound like an elitist argument. It's actually quite the opposite. I don't believe you should pay any attention to what art experts consider to be good or bad. But you may find that eventually much of what you like will be the "good" stuff.

The *British Journal of Aesthetics* published an interesting study that supports this idea. The researchers asked participants to review and rate the landscapes of two artists: the English pre-Raphaelite painter John Everett Millais (considered "good") and the contemporary painter Thomas Kinkade (considered "bad"). What they found was that the more participants were exposed to Millais' work, the more they liked it. And the more participants were exposed to Kinkade's work, the less they liked it.

John Everett Millais, *Autumn Leaves*

Thomas Kinkade, *Cobblestone Bridge*

Again, I'm not saying that there is anything wrong with liking Kinkade. I'm saying only that after you've studied a thousand landscape paintings, it is unlikely that his work will satisfy you.

A true art lover is not a snob. He does not think in terms of what is "right" or what is "smart." He's stimulated by visual imagery. He can't stop himself from looking at it. It doesn't matter whether it hangs in a museum or in a coffee shop, whether it is framed or unframed, famous or unknown, bought or found, made by man or nature. And it certainly doesn't matter if the critics approve of it.

Having a rich mind is all about the cultivation of aesthetic pleasure. And there are so many pleasures you can get from art.

Art can describe things...

I love the work of the early Dutch painter Hieronymus Bosch. I like the imagery in his murals and triptychs. I particularly like his grotesque depictions of hell, showing the many ways sinners will be tortured for eternity.

Hieronymus Bosch, *Hell 2*

I love looking at 15th, 16th, and 17th century Flemish paintings
of everyday life, as well. Van Eyck... Brueghel... Rubens...
They give me a window into a different time, a world that no
longer exists. I like to see what the people are doing, how they are
dressed, and the tools they work with.

Rogier van der Weyden, *Magdalen Reading*
(fragment of an altarpiece)

Quentin Matsys, *The Moneylender and his Wife*

Peter Paul Rubens, *Hélène Fourment in a Fur Coat*

Art can tell a story…

Do you remember how, when you were very young, you could read a story over and over again without any decrease in the pleasure it gave you? That's how I feel when I look at the work of figurative painters like Andrew Wyeth and Norman Rockwell.

Andrew Wyeth, *Public Sale*

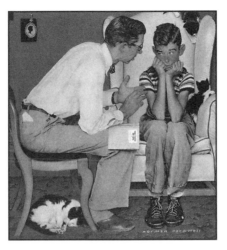

Norman Rockwell (*title unknown*)

Art can make a statement...

Henri Rousseau, *Snake Charmer*

Art can stir up thoughts or feelings…

Mary Cassatt, *The Manicure*

Art can inspire…

Edgar Degas, *The Little Fourteen-Year-Old Dancer*

How to Bring Art Into Your Life

As I said, you don't need to study art history to appreciate art.
You need only to look at it with conscious attention. Let the image
sink in. Be aware of how it makes you feel. Does it stimulate
any random thoughts or memories? You are not looking for

explanations. You are simply paying attention to your experience. That's all you have to do. Start with that and keep at it. The pleasure you get will increase and diversify as you look at more and more pieces.

Where to look? Anywhere. Everywhere. Not just on museum walls or in sculpture gardens or in books. In restaurants and shops. In government offices and private homes. Outside in parks and on billboards. On benches and on the sidewalk.

If you see something interesting, don't be afraid to check it out. Even if it means you have to ask permission to approach it.

And when you do visit museums, avoid the most common mistakes:

• Don't try to "do" the whole museum.

Some people feel that they have to see *everything*. They will spend three or four hours rushing through the galleries, barely glancing at the art.

As much as I enjoy art, it takes energy to appreciate it. So when I visit a museum, no matter how big it is, I plan to spend no more than 90 minutes there. That means deciding beforehand what I am going to look at.

You can do that by looking through a museum brochure or speaking to someone at the information desk. Don't feel compelled to see the current exhibition or the best-known pieces. Pick something that you think you will like.

• Don't spend more time reading the labels than looking at the art.

I hate people that do this. It tells me that they don't get it. That they are posers, wannabes. It pisses me off.

Spend a moment taking in all the paintings within eyeshot. Then go only to those that attract you. Spend as much time as you want looking at each one. Think about whether you like it or not. Or have mixed feelings. Feel the feelings. Think the thoughts. But don't try to make too much of them.

Look at the label only after you feel like you have "taken in" the piece. If you are surprised or intrigued by what you find out (the artist, when the piece was created, the medium), go back and look at it again.

• **When viewing special exhibits, try not to read the critical commentary—some "expert's" explanation of what you are looking at.**

Art criticism is generally biased, pompous, or just plain silly. Art criticism of modern art is 99 percent pretentious bullshit.

• **Finally, as former Met director Thomas Hoving said in an interview in *Attaché* magazine: "Don't feel you have to *get it*."**

"Modern and contemporary art, in particular, isn't supposed to be an intelligence test," said Hoving. "A Morris Louis is beautiful colors coming together. It doesn't mean anything. It's not supposed to."

Chapter 17

Richness From Music

The Philistine believes that appreciating music requires a multi-thousand-dollar investment in a state-of-the-art sound system. The man with the rich mind understands that what determines his musical enjoyment is not the quality of the equipment but the quality of the music itself.

By that I mean the subtlety, complexity, and emotional power of the musical score combined with the technical quality of the performance.

Everyone has a right to like any sort of music. But that doesn't mean all music is equally capable of providing a rich auditory experience.

I do think that some forms of music are "richer" than others. The criteria are, as I suggested above, subtlety, complexity, and emotional power.

If you accept those criteria, it shouldn't be difficult to agree that some forms of music (e.g., classical) are generally better than others (pop). But within any musical genre there are some pieces that are more complex, subtle, and emotionally powerful than others.

Because rich music is both complex and subtle, it tends to be an acquired taste. One of my friends recently told me that when he began to listen to classical music, he found Johann Sebastian Bach's to be "boring." So boring, he said, that he would often fall asleep while listening to it. But since Bach is generally considered to be a genius, he made an effort to appreciate his music. He listened to it almost every day for months, until one day something changed inside him.

The point is: If the music itself is complex, subtle, and emotionally powerful, you can acquire a taste for it. And once you acquire that taste, you can enjoy a lifetime of listening to music of many kinds.

Toward that end, I compiled several lists of "top ten" suggestions for you.

By the way… while going through the process of whittling down much larger lists of critically recommended favorites, I realized how insane "top ten" lists are. I could have easily created five top ten lists for each category. Still, if you are looking to venture into new musical territory, these will get you started.

Classical

1.   Beethoven's *Symphony No. 5*—the most famous piece of classical music ever written

2.   Mozart's *Piano Concertos 20* and *21*

3.   Beethoven's *Pathétique* and *Moonlight* piano sonatas

4.   Bach's *Brandenburg Concertos*

5.   Brahms' *Piano Trio No. 1*

6.   Stravinsky's *The Rite of Spring*

7.   Schubert's *Death and the Maiden* string quartet

8.   Tchaikovsky's *Pathétique* symphony

9.   Haydn's *Lord Nelson Mass*

10. Rachmaninoff's *Piano Concerto No. 2*

Opera

1.   Mozart's *The Marriage of Figaro*

2.   Bizet's *Carmen*

3.   Verdi's *Rigoletto*

4. Puccini's *Tosca*

5. Beethoven's *Fidelio*

6. Debussy's *Pelléas et Mélisande*

7. Janácek's *The Cunning Little Vixen*

8. Berg's *Wozzeck*

9. Tchaikovsky's *Eugene Onegin*

10. Massenet's *Werther*

Jazz

1. Duke Ellington's *Take the A Train*

2. John Coltrane's *My Favorite Things*

3. Miles Davis' *All Blues*

4. Stan Getz & Astrud Gilberto's *The Girl From Ipanema*

5. Benny Goodman's *Sing, Sing, Sing*

6. Dizzy Gillespie's *A Night in Tunisia*

7. Dave Brubeck's *Blue Rondo à la Turk*

8. Oliver Nelson's *Stolen Moments*

9. Louis Armstrong's *West End Blues*

10. Billie Holiday's *God Bless the Child*

Rock and Roll

1. Bob Dylan's *Like a Rolling Stone*

2. The Rolling Stones' *(I Can't Get No) Satisfaction*

3. The Beach Boys' *Good Vibrations*

4. Chuck Berry's *Maybellene*

5. The Beatles' *I Want to Hold Your Hand*

6. Ray Charles' *What'd I Say*

7. The Who's *My Generation*

8. Sam Cooke's *A Change Is Gonna Come*

9. Jimi Hendrix's *Purple Haze*

10. Elvis Presley's *Hound Dog*

Country

1. Burl Ives' *Cowboy's Lament (Streets of Laredo)*

2. George Jones' *White Lightning*

3. Tammy Wynette's *Stand By Your Man*

4. Willie Nelson's *Always on My Mind*

5. Johnny Cash's *I Walk the Line*

6. Tennessee Ernie Ford's *Sixteen Tons*

7. Garth Brooks' *The Dance*

8. Hank Williams Sr.'s *I'm So Lonesome I Could Cry*

9. Marty Robbins' *El Paso*

10. Patsy Cline's *Crazy*

Rhythm/Blues

1. The Temptations' *My Girl*

2. Amy Winehouse's *Back to Black*

3. Otis Redding's *The Dock of the Bay*

4. Marvin Gaye's *Let's Get It On*

5. Sam Cooke's *A Change Is Gonna Come*

6. The Commodores' *Just to Be Close to You*

7. Harold Melvin & the Blue Notes' *If You Don't Know Me by Now*

8. James Brown's *Say It Loud*

9. Percy Sledge's *When a Man Loves a Woman*

10. Prince's *Little Red Corvette*

Folk

1. Woody Guthrie's *This Land Is Your Land*

2. Bob Dylan's *Blowin' in the Wind*

3. Steve Goodman's *City of New Orleans*

4. Pete Seeger's *If I Had a Hammer*

5. The Kingston Trio's *Where Have All the Flowers Gone*

6. Leonard Cohen's *Suzanne*

7. Joni Mitchell's *The Circle Game*

8. Bob Dylan's *Don't Think Twice, It's All Right*

9. Joan Baez's *Diamonds and Rust*

10. Simon & Garfunkel's *Sounds of Silence*

Chapter 18

Richness From Reading

I cannot live without books.

— Thomas Jefferson

I grew up in a family of readers. My mother could easily (and often did) read a book a day. My father was a Shakespearean scholar who taught speed-reading on the side. If you walked through our house on any day at any time, you'd find several people reading. Reading, we all believed, was an essential part of a rich and productive life.

I believe that still. And I will tell you why.

How Reading Can Make You Smarter

Reading makes you smarter. In fact, it makes you smarter in almost every way you can be smart.

Studies show that people who read on a regular basis have higher raw intelligence, better analytical skills, stronger perceptive powers, and perform better when it comes to intellectual challenges.

If that were not enough, reading also improves *emotional* intelligence. In one study, participants read excerpts from literary fiction, popular fiction, or nonfiction. A control group read nothing at all. They were then given tests that measured their "social perception"—i.e., their ability to intuit things about people based on visual and verbal clues. Those who read literary fiction scored highest. Those who read nonfiction scored second-highest. Those who read popular fiction scored third-highest. And those who didn't read came in last. Two studies conducted by York University psychologist Raymond Mar, targeting both adults and children, came to the same conclusion.

Reading also improves memory. More than a dozen studies have demonstrated that regular readers are better at recalling all sorts of details—not just in the material they read but in every area of their lives.

And it improves analytical thinking—the ability to spot patterns in complex problems and conceive solutions.

It doesn't surprise me that reading makes you smarter. What surprises me is that some people think reading is an anachronistic skill. "I watch lots of biographies on the History Channel," one friend tells me. "I don't need to read books."

I'll grant my friend that there are plenty of good programs on TV these days. And there is no faster way to do quick research than by using Google. But watching TV or Googling does not activate the brain as fully and effectively as reading does.

How Reading Can Make You Healthier

Anything that makes you smarter is—as far as I'm concerned—something that any person interested in a rich and rewarding life should want to do. But reading offers health benefits too.

For one thing, reading is a very effective way to overcome stress. In a British study, participants engaged in an anxiety-provoking activity and then either read for a few minutes, listened to music, or played video games. The stress levels of those who read dropped 67 percent—more than any of the other groups. And, in fact, research conducted at the University of Sussex showed that reading is better at reducing stress than listening to music, enjoying a cup of tea or coffee, and even taking a walk.

A second health benefit you'll get from regular reading is a youthful brain. A study of 294 participants published in the journal *Neurology* found that those who engaged in mentally stimulating activities (such as reading) experienced slower memory decline. And according to research published in the journal *Proceedings of the National Academy of Sciences*, readers are less likely to have Alzheimer's disease.

"The brain is an organ just like every other organ in the body. It ages in regard to how it is used," lead author Dr. Robert P. Friedland told *USA Today*. "Just as physical activity strengthens the heart, muscles, and bones, intellectual activity strengthens the brain against disease."

Another study, reported in *Prevention* magazine, found that readers have a 32 percent slower rate of cognitive decline later in life.

"Brainy pursuits make the brain more efficient by changing its structure to continue functioning properly in spite of age-related neuropathologies," Robert S. Wilson, Ph.D., professor of neuropsychology at Rush University Medical Center, told the magazine.

How Reading Can Make You Kinder

Smarter and healthier—surely those are sufficient reasons to become an avid reader. But in doing my research for this book, I discovered yet another benefit. According to several studies, reading can actually make you kinder.

Researchers in the Netherlands, for example, found that people who were "emotionally transported" by a work of fiction experienced a boost in empathy.

Another study by the National Endowment for the Arts found that people who regularly read are much more likely to be engaged civically and culturally.

And yet another study, published in *Creativity Research Journal,* showed that people who have just read a short story have less need for "cognitive closure" than people who've just read a nonfiction essay. One hundred University of Toronto students read either one of eight short stories or one of eight essays. Then each student completed a survey measuring their emotional need for certainty and stability. Those who had read a short story had significantly lower scores than those who had read an essay. They expressed greater comfort with uncertainty and chaos—an attitude that allows for higher-level thinking and greater creativity.

Making "Rich" Choices

Some novels—think Danielle Steele or John Grisham—are easy to read and loads of fun (if you like that sort of thing), but provide no lasting pleasures. You read them quickly, caught up in the plot or amused by certain well-drawn characters. But then you put the books down and forget about them. You've invested time into them and you've gotten a return on your investment, but the return was very modest.

Compare that experience to reading *Sophie's Choice* or *Lolita*, books that are more "difficult." Such books challenge you on every level. The authors' writing styles are more sophisticated. Their plots are less conventional. Their characters are multifaceted, like people tend to be in real life. And there are ideas presented throughout the story—ideas that often test your convictions and notions and beliefs.

You will get some of the benefits of reading—especially stress reduction—no matter what kind of books you read. But if you want a life that is richer in terms of your emotional and intellectual experience, you have to be selective in your choices. As with music and art, that means choosing books that have complexity, subtlety, and emotional power.

I don't have the space or time to recommend great books for every aspect of a rich life, so I will limit my suggestions to five categories: modern fiction, classical fiction, short stories, nonfiction, and poetry.

My recommendations are in no way meant to be definitive. As award-winning author Lloyd Alexander said, "We don't need to have just one favorite. We keep adding favorites. Our favorite book is always the book that speaks most directly to us at a particular stage in our lives. And our lives change. We have other favorites that give us what we most need at that particular time. But we never lose the old favorites. They're always with us. We just sort of accumulate them."

My 10 Favorite Modern Novels

1. *Lolita* by Vladimir Nabokov

2. *The Old Man and the Sea* by Ernest Hemingway

3. *The Road* by Cormac McCarthy

4. *True Grit* by Charles Portis

5. *One Flew Over the Cuckoo's Nest* by Ken Kesey

6. *On the Road* by Jack Kerouac

7. *Sophie's Choice* by William Styron

8. *Naked Lunch* by William Burroughs

9. *To Kill a Mockingbird* by Harper Lee

10. *The Great Gatsby* by F. Scott Fitzgerald

My 10 Favorite Classics

1. *The Adventures of Huckleberry Finn* by Mark Twain

2. *Pride and Prejudice* by Jane Austen

3. *A Tale of Two Cities* by Charles Dickens

4. *The Tin Drum* by Günter Grass

5. *Wuthering Heights* by Emily Brontë

6. *Moby-Dick* by Herman Melville

7. *Brave New World* by Aldous Huxley

8. *Lucky Jim* by Kingsley Amis

9. *Invisible Man* by Ralph Ellison

10. *Native Son* by Richard Wright

My 10 Favorite Short Story Collections

1. *Dubliners* by James Joyce

2. *A Good Scent From a Strange Mountain* by Robert Olen Butler

3. *Nothing Gold Can Stay* by Ron Rash

4. *What We Talk About When We Talk About Love* by Raymond Carver

5. *The Complete Short Stories of O. Henry*

6. *Men Without Women* by Ernest Hemingway

7. *The Complete Stories of Edgar Allan Poe*

8. *Will You Please Be Quiet, Please?* by Raymond Carver

9. *A History of the World in 10 ½ Chapters* by Julian Barnes

10. *Pastoralia* by George Saunders

My 10 Favorite Nonfiction Books

1. *Ten Philosophical Mistakes* by Mortimer J. Adler

2. *Economics in One Lesson* by Henry Hazlitt

3. *The Elements of Style* by Strunk & White

4. *The Painted Word* by Tom Wolfe

5. *Zen and the Art of Motorcycle Maintenance* by Robert M. Pirsig

6. *Out of Africa* by Isak Dinesen

7. *A Moveable Feast* by Ernest Hemingway

8. *The Essays of Michel de Montaigne*

9. *In Cold Blood* by Truman Capote

10. *The American Language* by H.L. Mencken

My 10 Favorite Poetry Books

1. *Shakespeare's Sonnets*

2. *Selected Poems: Edna St. Vincent Millay*

3. *The Waste Land and Other Poems* by T.S. Eliot

4. *Howl and Other Poems* by Allen Ginsberg

5. *Selected Poems of Ezra Pound*

6. *The Collected Poems of William Butler Yeats*

7. *Selected Poems by W. H. Auden*

8. *The Complete Poems of Emily Dickinson*

9. *Love Is a Dog From Hell* by Charles Bukowski

10. *The Collected Works of Robert Penn Warren*

No matter how busy you may think you are, you must find time for reading, or surrender yourself to self-chosen ignorance.

— Confucius

Chapter 19

Richness From Movies

There is a Chinese proverb that goes something like this: "Pearls don't lie on the seashore. If you want one, you have to dive for it."

In Part II of this book, I've been applying that observation to the way we choose to spend our time—at work and at play.

I've argued that to enjoy a full, rewarding life, you must spend your work time focusing on projects you value and your leisure time on activities that somehow challenge you and improve you as a person.

For lack of a more precise term, we categorize more challenging books and music and art as "better." But what makes one book or symphony or painting better than another?

I've said that there are three qualities that are usually present in "better" literature and music and art: complexity, subtlety, and emotional power.

Think about that for a moment. Complexity. Subtlety. Emotional power. Dealing with complexity requires a sharp mind. Dealing with subtlety requires attentive eyes and ears. Taking in something that has emotional power requires emotional resilience.

By "complexity," I don't mean complicated. I don't mean, for example, a book with a plot line that has 17 different threads running through it. I mean that there is something in the work that goes deeper than the surface and encompasses more than the obvious.

Hemingway's *The Old Man and the Sea* has a very simple plot line: A poor fisherman goes out to sea, catches a huge fish, and is unable to get it back to shore before it is decimated by sharks. But the story itself is so much more than that. By the time you've finished reading this very slim book, you feel like you understand in some deep way not only this man but also something more about poverty and nobility and human grace.

By subtlety, I mean something like the opposite of obvious. I mean that the subject matter is treated with delicacy and precision. The artist/writer/composer is not satisfied with presenting the obvious. He wants to convey the complexity he sees in his subject matter in an understated way. He does this so the viewer/reader/listener can discover the complexity on his own.

The third criterion, emotional power, denotes something more than the capacity to provoke an immediate emotional response (fear/pity/sympathy). The objective—if you can say that there is an objective—is to elicit a response that is both deep and enduring. To leave the viewer/reader/listener a slightly different person than he was before.

In discussing art, literature, and music, I've said that you can make your mental/emotional life richer by choosing to spend your leisure time with works that have complexity, subtlety, and emotional power.

The same criteria apply to movies. (I'm going to focus on movies—but everything I say here will apply equally well to TV shows.)

Most movies—certainly most movies made in Hollywood—are made to be fast-paced and fun to watch. Whether it's a thriller starring Harrison Ford or a comedy starring Adam Sandler, the producer's goal is to sell tickets.

This is true even for many movies that win awards. Take the most obvious relatively recent example: *Titanic*. It was a major motion picture that won 11 Academy Awards. You don't need to be a film snob to see that *Titanic* had near-zero complexity, zero subtlety, and that any emotional power it had was the kind Hallmark cards are known for.

You may have liked *Titanic*. But liking a movie is not necessarily a criterion for judging its ability to enrich you.

Movies, like food, come in many degrees of quality. Some movies are like junk food—they provide temporary satisfaction. But that satisfaction sometimes turns to other emotions (regret, guilt, anger) after you have indulged. And a steady diet of such fare will leave your mind flabby.

Good movies, like good books, do more than tell stories. They provoke your thinking, challenging you to go deeper and further with ideas than you otherwise might. They inflame your aesthetic sensibility, even if you never thought you had one. And when they are very good, they can change or deepen your perspective... and, in doing so, enrich your life.

That said, here are some movies that I strongly recommend. Keep in mind that these recommendations are based on the movies I've seen, which represents only a fraction of the good movies out there.

My Top 20 Classic Movies

- *All About Eve*
- *Sunrise: A Song of Two Humans*
- *Casablanca*
- *The Maltese Falcon*
- *The Wizard of Oz*
- *The Bridge on the River Kwai*
- *To Kill a Mockingbird*
- *Rear Window*
- *The Third Man*
- *Vertigo*

- *Psycho*

- *Some Like It Hot*

- *Sunset Boulevard*

- *Gone With the Wind*

- *The African Queen*

- *Double Indemnity*

- *Rebel Without a Cause*

- *City Lights*

- *Frankenstein*

- *Lawrence of Arabia*

My Top 20 Modern Movies

- *The Godfather, Part I*

- *Pulp Fiction*

- *Apocalypse Now*

- *The Conversation*

- *Bonnie and Clyde*

- *Taxi Driver*

- *Schindler's List*

- *Five Easy Pieces*

- *The Deer Hunter*

- *Reservoir Dogs*

- *Slum Dog Millionaire*

- *Amadeus*

- *The French Connection*

- *The Graduate*

- *Jaws*

- *One Flew Over the Cuckoo's Nest*

- *American Graffiti*

- *Easy Rider*

- *Goodfellas*

- *The Godfather, Part II*

My Top 20 Foreign Language Films

- *La Dolce Vita* (Italian)

- *8½* (Italian)

- *Breathless* (French)

- *M* (German)

- *The Discreet Charm of the Bourgeoisie* (French)

- *The Seven Samurai* (Japanese)

- *My Night at Maud's* (French)

- *The 400 Blows* (French)

- *Flowers of Shanghai* (Chinese)

- *The Bicycle Thief* (Italian)

- *The Hunt* (Danish)

- *Amour* (French)

- *The Baader Meinhof Complex* (German)

- *Departures* (Japanese)

- *The Lives of Others* (German)

- *The Sea Inside* (Spanish)

- *Amélie* (French)

- *Crouching Tiger, Hidden Dragon* (Chinese)

- *Tsotsi* (South African)

- *Footnote* (Israeli)

You can easily develop your own lists—and I urge you to do it. Start with mine and get on the Internet to find some others. Don't be surprised when you find that most of these lists overlap. There's a reason some movies are consistently rated at the top. It is because they are—compared to the average movie—more complex, subtle, and emotionally powerful.

Then set some time aside to watch these movies, one after the other. Don't feel compelled to like them just because other people do. And don't feel compelled to watch any movie all the way through. Give it at least twenty minutes. If you're not involved by then, go on to the next one.

The idea is to be your own judge. And the criteria should not be how "easy" or "fun" it was to watch a particular movie but how it affected you afterward. Did it give you a new view on some aspect of life? Did it teach you something interesting that helps you understand how things work? Did it stimulate your thinking?

The goal is to build your own list of movies that you can watch again and again… getting more out of them each and every time you do.

In Conclusion

A hundred years ago, luxury goods of any kind were out of the financial reach of 99 percent of the population. But today, thanks to industrialization, globalization, and information technology, a middle-class income is enough to enjoy the best that life has to offer.

In Part I of this book, I made the argument that the finest material things can be part of your experience if you spend your money wisely. In other words, if you make buying decisions based on quality and cost of use.

In Part II, I argued that, although luxurious things comprise a part of living rich, the bigger and more important part is how you spend your time. We all—billionaires and minimum-wage workers alike—have the same allotment. We are all given 24 hours a day, 168 hours a week, and 52 weeks a year. How we fill that time is the most important factor in determining the richness of our experience.

We sometimes think that we don't have the luxury of choosing how we will spend our hours. But I believe we do. And I hope I have convinced you that this is true for you. I also hope I have shown you how you can start living each of your 24 daily hours as richly and as freely as a billionaire.

Featured Books From Cap & Bells Press

To order these books, visit www.amazon.com

America in Still Life: Barnett Greenberg

By Donald Mahoney, Mark Morgan Ford, and Timothy Sullivan

Barnett George Greenberg was an unknown artist destined to be forgotten... until Donald Mahoney and Mark Morgan Ford came upon a cache of his work. Impressed by the quality of what Greenberg had left behind, they tried to find out more about the man. What they discovered was a remarkable life.

Back and Out Again

Poems by Mark Morgan Ford

This is Mark Morgan Ford's first collection of poetry—an exploration of the possibilities of rhyme, rhythm, and form inspired by his interest in everything from mythology to politics to the complexities of human relationships.

Back From the Abyss: The Autobiography of a Low-Bottom Alky

By Kieran Doherty

With a voice reminiscent of Pete Hamill's in *A Drinking Life* and a childhood as tough as Frank McCourt's in *Angela's Ashes*, Kieran tells his story, full of wit, bravado, and Irish charm.

A Joyous Fatalism

By Timothy Siniscalchi, with photographs by Gwen Gove

Why a book of aphorisms written by a contemporary, unknown author? Because we believe the aphorism is a valuable literary species. And without the publication of new aphorisms by new writers, the species cannot survive. That said, we introduce you to Timothy Siniscalchi...

Books About Copywriting by Mark Morgan Ford From American Writers & Artists Inc.

To order these books, visit:
http://www.awaionline.com/livingrich/awaibooks/

The Architecture of Persuasion: How to Write Well-Constructed Sales Letters
By Michael Masterson*

Copy Logic! The New Science of Producing Breakthrough Copy (Without Criticism)
By Michael Masterson* and Mike Palmer

Great Leads: The Six Easiest Ways to Start Any Sales Message
By Michael Masterson* and John Forde

Persuasion: The Subtle Art of Getting What You Want
By Mark Morgan Ford and Will Newman

Also available from AWAI:

Wealth Planning for Freelancers, a program by Michael Masterson*

Additional Books
by Mark Morgan Ford

To order these books, visit: www.amazon.com

Automatic Wealth: The 6 Steps to Financial Independence
By Michael Masterson*
John Wiley & Sons, Publisher

Automatic Wealth for Grads… and Anyone Else Just Starting Out
By Michael Masterson*
John Wiley & Sons, Publisher

Changing the Channel: 12 Easy Ways to Make Millions for Your Business
By Michael Masterson* and Maryellen Tribby
John Wiley & Sons, Publisher

The Pledge: Your Master Plan for an Abundant Life
By Michael Masterson*
John Wiley & Sons, Publisher

Power and Persuasion: How to Command Success in Business and Your Personal Life
By Michael Masterson*
John Wiley & Sons, Publisher

Ready, Fire, Aim: Zero to $100 Million in No Time Flat
By Michael Masterson*
John Wiley & Sons, Publisher

The Reluctant Entrepreneur: Turning Dreams Into Profits
By Michael Masterson*
John Wiley & Sons, Publisher

Seven Years to Seven Figures: The Fast-Track Plan to Becoming a Millionaire
By Michael Masterson*
John Wiley & Sons, Publisher

*Michael Masterson is a pen name for Mark Morgan Ford

Cap & Bells is a boutique publishing company that focuses on contemporary fiction, nonfiction, poetry, and art books. Launched in 2012, it is our mission to be a vehicle for undiscovered writers and to keep the art of storytelling alive.

Visit www.capandbellspress.com to find out more about our books and to sign up for our mailing list.

CAP &
BELLS
PRESS